FOR
YOUTH GROUPS

Other books by the authors:

Called to Care
Far-Out Ideas for Youth Groups
Fun-N-Games
Good Clean Fun
Great Ideas for Small Youth Groups
Greatest Skits on Earth
High School Ministry
Holiday Ideas for Youth Groups
Ideas for Social Action
Incredible Ideas for Youth Groups
Junior High Ministry
Play It! Great Games for Groups
Right-On Ideas for Youth Groups
Super Ideas for Youth Groups
Tension Getters
Tension Getters II
Way-Out Ideas for Youth Groups
Youth Specialties Clip Art Book

Super ideas
FOR
YOUTH GROUPS

Mike Yaconelli & Wayne Rice

Youth Specialties

ZONDERVAN PUBLISHING HOUSE
Grand Rapids, Michigan

SUPER IDEAS FOR YOUTH GROUPS
Copyright © 1979 by The Zondervan Corporation

Youth Specialties Books are published by Zondervan
Publishing House, 1415 Lake Drive, S.E.,
Grand Rapids, Michigan 49506

Library of Congress Cataloging in Publication Data
Rice, Wayne.
    Super ideas for youth groups.

    1. Games.   2. Youth—Recreation.   I. Yaconelli, Mike,
joint author.   II. Title.
GV1201.R444   790.19'2   79-17410
ISBN 0-310-34981-8

Printed in the United States of America

86 87 88 89 90 / 16 15 14 13 12 11 10

The authors wish to thank the many churches,
youth groups, youth organizations and workers,
whose creativity made this book possible.

Contents

CHRISTMAS CONFUSION

This idea is based on "Confusion" found in *Far-out Ideas for Youth Groups* (p. 9). It is a great crowd breaker for parties or socials. Simply give everyone in your group a copy of the instructions below. Read over the instructions to the group to make sure they understand them. The object is to finish all the instructions correctly before anyone else. The first one finished can receive a prize of some kind. There is no correct order so the instructions can be completed in whatever order you want.

1. Get five autographs on the back of this sheet (first, middle, last names).

2. Find three other people and sing together, "We Wish You A Merry Christmas" as loudly as you can. Then initial each other's papers here. _____   _____ _____

3. Tell someone the names of three of Santa's reindeer. Then have that person initial here. _____

4. You play Santa Claus. Find someone of the opposite sex, sit him or her on your lap and ask what he or she wants for Christmas. Then have him or her initial here. _____

5. Pick the ornament on the Christmas tree which you like the best. Find someone else and give him a 15 second speech on why you like that particular ornament. Then have that person initial here. _____

6. You are Ebenezer Scrooge. Find someone and ask him to wish you a Merry Christmas. When he does, say, "Bah! Humbug!" ten times while jumping up and down. Then have that person initial here._____

7. Leapfrog over someone wearing red or green. Then have him initial here. __

9

8. Find someone of the opposite sex and have him whistle one verse of "Away In A Manger" to you. Then have that person initial here. _____

CORK GAME

Here's a good "get acquainted" game. Have your group sit in a circle with one less chair than there are participants. Everyone seated is required to learn the full name of the people on either side of him. One person is left in the middle of the circle. The person in the middle then approaches any person seated, points to him, says "left" or "right," and then counts to ten. The person pointed to must give the first and last name of the one on the left or right. If the one pointed to does not give the correct name, a black cork mark is put on his face and he must change places with the one in the middle. If the person pointed to does give the correct name, the person in the middle gets the black mark on his face.

Every once in a while, the leader yells, "switch," and everyone must exchange seats by going to the opposite side of the circle. One person will end up without a seat and receives a black mark. Each person seated, quickly learns the name of the people on either side and the game continues.

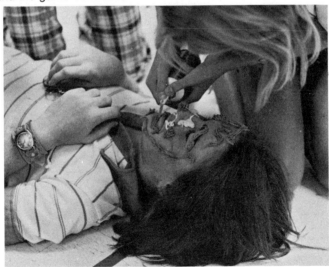

FACE DECORATING

Have several couples participate in this one. Each girl is given items necessary for cake decorating (squeeze tubes of icing, whipped cream, candy sprinkles, etc.) and they decorate their guy partner's face. The boy should lie down on his back. When finished, the guys stand and have their faces judged, either by the audience or a panel of judges.

GETTING TO KNOW YOU

Give everyone in your group a copy of the chart below. Each person attempts to get people to sign a box containing a description that *truthfully* describes them. The first person to get all the boxes signed, or after a reasonable time, the one with the most boxes signed wins. People can sign more than one box if the description truthfully describes them.

I feel like my breath is bad.	I am madly in love with someone in this room.	On a scale of ten, my sex appeal is about a 3.	The last date I went on was real bad.
I have dandruff.	I am on a diet.	I am good looking, but not conceited.	I want to be President of the U.S.
I have seriously considered trading my folks in on a new stereo.	Basically, my brother/sister is a turkey.	I am afraid of the dark.	I think school is a waste of time.
I don't like my voice. It's too high.	I have B.O. a lot.	I am going to be famous someday.	All of my teeth are not real.

The winner as described above, then reads back to the group the signers and the description they signed under. It creates a lot of laughs.

IDENTITY

As your group enters the room, have each fill out a name tag and drop it in a basket. After everyone has arrived, have them stand in a circle. Pass the basket around and have each person take a name tag (not his name) without letting everyone else see the name.

Then have everyone turn to the left and place the name tag he is holding on the back of the person standing in front of him. The object of the game is for each person to discover the name printed on the name tag pinned to his back. He finds out his identity by asking questions that can be answered "yes" or "no." Questions like, "Do I have red hair?" or "Am I wearing jeans?" Each kid can only ask two questions of each person he meets.

When people discover whose name they have, they then go to that person, place their hands on his/her shoulders and proceed to follow him/her around the room. As more people discover their identity, the lines of people with hands on shoulders will lengthen until the last person finds his identity.

LET ME INTRODUCE MYSELF

Here's a crowd breaker idea for youth who know each other somewhat. Have each person write a short paragraph on himself using the pronoun "I." Tell them to be somewhat vague and to try and hide their identity, but to be truthful. Hand the paragraphs to a "reader" who will then read the paragraphs and allow the others in the groups to discuss each paragraph and then guess the writer's identity. Of course, the person who wrote the paragraph will have to remain elusive during the discussion. The object is to try and fool the group, which encourages kids to share things about themselves not already known. This works best with a group of about ten.

MOOING CONTEST

Send two people out of the room after telling them that they are to be judges in a "mooing contest." After they are both out of earshot, take the entire group into confidence and explain that this is a trick to be played on one of the two volunteers (person number one). The object is to get him to "moo" loudly all by himself after his turn at judging. Go through the entire instructions beforehand, even to the point of rehearsing the moos. The steps are as follows:

1. Person number one comes back in the room and stands in the center of the circle where he is told that he is to judge which member of the group is the loudest after

the group moos three times. He is told the group has chosen a mooer to be the one and he must try to guess who he is. The group then moos once, then a second time, then a third time and person number one is asked who the loudest mooer is. By common consent whoever he picks is wrong and another is offered (usually a quieter person) as the real loudest mooer. So person number one loses.

2. Then person number one rejoins the group (sits down in the audience). The leader says the groups must now pick another loudest mooer. After suggesting several (they all decline) the leader fakes that he has a novel idea and asks person number one to be the loudest mooer—for person number two would never guess him. Others join in support of the idea and person number one is rehearsed several times as the loudest mooer of the group (until he's really bellowing).

3. Here's the trick. When person number two comes into the circle, he's told to listen for the loudest mooer. The leader counts 1, 2, 3 and all moo once. He counts again and all moo the second time. He counts again and all take a deep breath, but *don't moo*—and you will then hear a great solo moo from person number one. He is then awarded the Bull-calling award.

NAME SEARCH

The purpose of this is to get people who don't know each other to become familiar with the names of everyone in the group. Make sure there are no lists containing the names of the group anywhere visible; instead, put a large name tag on each person.

Give each person a word search puzzle with every person's name somewhere in the puzzle. Of course, to do the puzzle, people have to know the names they are looking for, which means there will be a lot of walking around and looking at name tags.

Sample: *Solution:*

K E U S O L D X N
A L L A N A R F V
T T O K R S J A D
H T E B A Z I L E
Y R G G L T Z R Y
R E T E P P L A K
M I J K H L R A C
T R S H A R O N W

SIGNATURES

This is a mixer that can be used with any age group. It's easy and fun to play. Give each person a sheet of paper and a pencil. Written down the left hand border of the paper are the letters in a word or phrase selected because of its association with the holiday or the occasion of the party. For example, at a Christmas party, the words written down the side might be "Merry Christmas."

On a signal, the players go around getting the signatures of the other players. They try to find someone whose first or last name begins with one of the letters in the key word or phrase. When someone is found, he is asked to sign next to the appropriate letter. The first person to get signatures next to all of the letters on his or her sheet is the winner. If no winner has come forth after a certain period of time, stop the game, and whoever has the most signatures found is the winner. In case of a tie, first names that match are worth more than last names—so the most matching first names wins. For larger groups, the phrase can be longer, or shorter for smaller groups.

SING SONG SORTING

This game is similar to "Barnyard" and is great as a way to divide a crowd into teams or small groups. Prepare ahead of time on small slips of paper an equal number of four (or however many groups you want) different song titles. As each person enters the room, he receives (at random) one of these song titles. In other words, if you had 100 kids and you wanted four teams, there would be 25 each of the four different songs. On a signal, the lights go out (if you do this at night) and each kid starts singing the song he received as loudly as possible. No talking or yelling, only singing. Each person tries to locate others singing the same song, and the first team to get together is the winner. Song titles should be well-known.

NAME THE NEIGHBORS

Here is a fun problem of logic that might come in handy sometime when you want to keep a group occupied:

Fran, Grace, Helen, Ida, and Jane and their husbands all live on a certain street that runs east to west in the town of Centerville. From the following clues, give each couple's full names and describe exactly where on the street each couple lives.

1. Grace has Ralph as one next door neighbor and the Greens as her other next door neighbor.
2. The Browns live in the westernmost house—Ned in the easternmost.
3. Sam has Ida as one next door neighbor and Peter as his next door neighbor on the other side.

4. Both Jane and Peter live east of the Whites.
5. Peter lives next door to the Blacks.
6. Tom lives west of the Greys, and east of Grace.
7. Helen and Jane are next door neighbors. The Greys live next to Jane also, but on the other side.

Solution: (from west to east on the street)

•Ralph+Ida Brown   •Sam+Grace White   •Peter+Helen Green   •Tom+Jane Black   •Ned+Fran Grey

S AND T

Divide the group down the middle. Have one side be the "S and T's" and the other side be the "Everything Else's." The idea is that you will count together as a group from one to twenty, and every time you say a number that begins with an "S" or a "T," the "S and T" group stands up. On all the other numbers, the "Everything Else" group stands up. Start slowly, then do it again a little faster. Each time the "Everything Else's" stand on "one," and the "S and T's" stand on "two and three," and so on. It really gets wild the faster you go.

To make more of a game out of this, have everyone sit in a circle, and start counting around the circle, "1, 2, 3, 4, etc." up to 20 and then start at "1" again, and so on. Every time a person says a number that begins with an S or T, he must stand up before saying it. If he doesn't, he is out of the game, and the game continues. The counting must be done in rhythm without waiting (or you are eliminated). It's very confusing, but lots of fun.

STATISTICAL TREASURE HUNT

Here is an exceptionally good game for getting groups acquainted. The game can be played around tables at banquet events. Divide group into teams of equal number, if possible. Give each team a typewritten or mimeographed sheet of questions which are to be answered and evaluated as indicated on the sheet. Each team appoints a captain who acts as the gleaner of information and recorder.

Below is a list of typical questions and methods of scoring. You may not want to use all of these. These may suggest other questions to you which may be more appropriate for your particular group or occasion.

General Questions:

_____ 1. Counting January as one point, February as two points and so on through the calendar year, add up the total of birthday points at your table. Just ask 'em what month they were born, not the year!

_____ 2. Counting one point for each different state named, give score for different number of birth states represented on your team.

_____ 3. Total of all shoe sizes added together. (One foot only.)

_____ 4. Total number of operations everyone at your table has had. Serious dental surgery counts, but not just an ordinary tooth pulling. You only have time to count the number, no time for all the interesting details!

_____ 5. Get your hair color score: Black counts two; brown counts one; blonde counts three; red counts five; gray counts three; white counts five.

_____ 6. Score a point for each self-made article worn or carried by your teammates.

_____ 7. Add the total number of miles traveled by each member to get to this meeting.

_____ 8. Total number of children teammates have. If husbands and wives are sitting together or are on one team, count their children only once. Score as follows: Each child counts one point; set of twins counts five points; grandchildren count three points each.

_____ 9. Score one point for each different college attended, but not necessarily graduated from.

STRING TIE MYSTERY

Here's a simple little game that you can use to test your group's creativity. Hang two strings from the ceiling in such a way that they dangle approximately one foot from the floor (both strings should be about the same length). The strings should be far enough apart that, while holding the dangling end of one string, the other string hanging down is a foot or so out of reach. Challenge anyone in you group to tie the dangling ends of the strings together with no help from the audience. The only thing that can be used in this task is an ordinary pair of pliers.

How is it done? Simple. Tie the pliers to the end of one of the string and then swing the string back and forth. Then hold the end of the other string, and when the pliers swing close enough, grab them. Untie the pliers and tie the two strings together.

UP AND DOWN BONNIE

Here's a great variation to the song, "My Bonnie Lies Over The Ocean." While singing the song, have everyone stand on the first word that begins with a "B" and sit down on the next word that begins with "B." Continue the same process on all the "B" words. For variation, have half the group start the song standing up. People get confused about whether they are to be standing or sitting. Lots of fun.

WHOPPER

This is an interesting activity for groups that know each other fairly well. Give each person the questionnaire below. Instruct everyone to tell the truth in answer to four of the questions, but to lie in response to one of the questions. The "whopper" should sound reasonable. After everyone is finished, each person then reads his answers to the rest of the group and they try to guess which answer is the "whopper."

Answer each of the five questions below. Tell the truth on four of them and tell a "whopper" on one.

1. Where were you born?

2. How many siblings (brothers and sisters, dummy) do you have?

3. What are your hobbies?

4. Where were you at 10:00 last Saturday night?

5. What do you hope to have as a career?

2 | Games

BACK TO BACK

Divide your group into pairs and have them sit on the floor back to back and link arms. Then tell them to stand up. With a little timing and sensitivity, it shouldn't be too hard. Then combine two pairs into a foursome. Have the foursome sit on the floor back to back with arms linked. Tell them to stand up. It is a little harder with four. Keep adding more people to the group until the giant blob can't stand up any more.

BEAN-BAG BALL

This is a wild game that is great for camps and can be set up like a championship "football" game. Divide the crowd into two large groups and give them names of schools (make them up). Each "school" is then provided plenty of newspapers, tape, magic markers, crepe paper, scissors, poster paint, etc. They then have thirty minutes or so to do the following:

1. Prepare a band, complete with uniforms (make them), instruments (anything you can find), drum major, majorettes, etc., plus a march or two that can be hummed (waxed paper on combs help here). Band should be prepared to play the "Star Spangled Banner."

2. Prepare cheerleaders (usually boys dressed like girls), complete with costumes, cheers, etc.

3. Prepare a Homecoming Queen with Court (could be boys or girls, or mixed). Fix up costumes.

4. Prepare a team for "Bean-Bag-Ball" (see following rules). Ordinarily a team of seven plus a coach will do.

5. Prepare a half-time program and a crowning of the Homecoming Queen and court.

After each school has done all this, then begin the action as follows:

1. School A Marching Band marches onto the field followed by the team and cheerleaders. An announcer introduces the team. The cheerleaders do their stuff.
2. School B does the same.
3. Leaders ask one band to play the "Star Spangled Banner."
4. First half of the game (5 to 7 minutes), cheerleaders and bands each root for their team.
5. Half-time program:
   School A's program and crowning of Queen.
   School B's program and crowning of Queen.
6. Second half of the game.
7. Victory celebration by the winning team.

Here's how "Bean-Bag-Ball" is played: Two referees are needed with whistles. The playing field can vary in size, but anything larger than a volleyball court will do. There should be a half-way line and at each end of the field a folding chair is placed three feet beyond the goal line. The rules are similar to basketball except the bag-holder may only take three steps with the bean bag, then he must pass it. Goals are scored by tossing the bean bag between the seat and the seatback of the chair. A good P.A. system and announcer will add a great deal.

BEDLAM

This game requires four teams of equal size. Each team takes one corner of the room or playing field. The play area can be either square or rectangular. On a signal (whistle, etc.), each team attempts to move as quickly as possible to the corner directly across from their corner (diagonally) performing an announced activity as they go. The first team to get all its members into its new corner wins that particular round. The first round can be simply running to the opposite corner, but after that you can use any number of possibilities: walking backward, wheelbarrow racing (one person is the wheelbarrow), piggyback, rolling somersaults, hopping on one foot, skipping, "crab walking", etc. There will be literally mass bedlam in the center as all four teams crisscross.

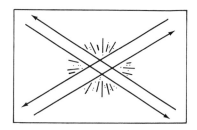

BLIND VOLLEYBALL

Divide the kids into two equal groups. The two teams then get on each side of a volleyball court and sit down either on chairs or on the floor in rows, like in regular volleyball. The "net" should be a solid divider that obstructs the view of the other team, such as blankets hung over a regular volleyball net or rope. The divider should also be low enough that players cannot see under it. Then play volleyball. Use a big, light plastic ball instead of a volleyball. Regular volleyball rules and boundaries apply. A player cannot stand up to hit the ball. The added dimension of the solid net gives a real surprise element to the game when the ball comes flying over the net.

CATASTROPHE

This game can be used with a group of 15 or more people. Divide the group into three teams, and have each team sit in chairs in three lines, parallel to each other and with about three feet between the teams. All players should be facing the same direction, toward the front of their team's line. (Each player sits facing a team-mate's back.)

Each team has the name of a town, such as "Pottstown," "Mudsville," and "Dry Gulch" (any name will do). Each player on each team is assigned an "occupation," such as plumber, carpenter, policeman, preacher, teacher, doctor, etc. There should be the same occupations on each team, and they should be seated in the same order on each team as well.

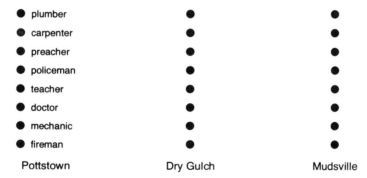

| Pottstown | Dry Gulch | Mudsville |

The leader then calls out an occupation and a town, such as, "We need a policeman at Pottstown." At that point, the policemen on each team must get up out of their chairs, run around their team and return to their chairs. The first person back in his or her chair wins a point for his or her team.

An additional twist to this game is that players must run around their teams in the right direction. This is determined by which town is called. For example, if the team lines are arranged so that Pottstown is on everyone's left, Mudsville is on the right, and Dry Gulch is in the middle, then if Mudsville is called, everyone must get out of their chairs on the right, and run around the team in a clockwise (right) direction. Pottstown would be left, and if Dry Gulch is called, either direction is okay. If you don't run in the correct direction, you lose.

If the leader calls out, "There's been a catastrophe in (town.)", then everyone on all three teams must get up and run around the team, again in the correct direction. The first team completely seated gets the point. Remember that team members must get up from their chairs on the correct side, as well as going around in the right direction.

CATCH THE WIND

Have one person lie on the floor with a straw in his mouth. At his head place a chair. A second person sits in the chair facing the person on the floor and has a party blower in his mouth. The chair back should be towards the person on the floor and the seated person should rest his chin on the chair back. A third person sits next to the person on the floor and places Kleenex (or any other brand) tissues one at a time on the end of the straw. The person on the floor then blows the tissue up in the air and the person in the chair tries to catch it with the party blower. This game requires three-person teams, obviously, and the winning team is the first to successfully catch a given number of tissues. The distance from the blower on the floor to the catcher may vary depending on the distance up that people can blow.

CHURCH TRIVIA

Divide the group into teams (or kids may compete individually) and give each a list of

22

unusual things in the church to identify. Here's a sample list:

1. The name of the company that manufactured the church's fire extinguisher.
2. The number of steps in the baptistry.
3. The number of fuses in the fuse box.
4. The location of the first-aid kit.
5. The last word in (A certain book in the church library).
6. The number of yellow lines painted on the parking lot.

Your list should include twenty or so items such as these. On "go," everyone tries to locate the various information required as quickly as possible. With teams, the questions can be assigned to the different team members. The first to finish, or the most questions correctly answered, wins.

CIRCLE SOCCER

Two teams get into one circle, half on one side and half on the other.

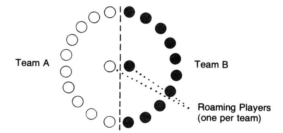

A ball is thrown into the circle and the players try to kick it out through the other team's side. If the ball is kicked out over the heads of the players, the point goes to the nonkicking team. If the ball is kicked out below the heads of the players, the kicking team gets the point. Hands may not be used at all, only feet and bodies. No one may move out of position except one player per team who may kick the ball to his teammates if the ball gets stuck in the center. He may not score, however, or cross into the other team's territory. If the roaming player gets hit with the ball (when kicked by the other team), the kicking team gets a point.

CLOTHESPIN CHALLENGE

Two contestants are selected and seated in chairs facing each other with their knees touching. Each is shown a large pile of clothespins at the right of his chair. Each is blindfolded and given 2 minutes to pin as many clothespins as possible on the pant legs of the other contestant.

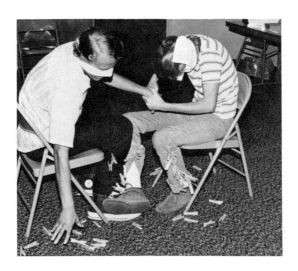

CLOTHES PINNING

Here's a wild game that is simple, yet fun to play with any size group. Give everyone in the group six clothespins. On "go," each player tries to pin his clothespins on other players' clothing. Each of your six pins must be hung on six different players. You must keep moving to avoid having clothespins hung on you, yet you try to hang your pins on someone else. When you hang all six of your clothespins, you remain in the game, but try to avoid having more pins hung on you. At the end of the time limit, the person with the least amount of clothespins hanging on him (or her) is the winner and the person with the most is the loser.

Another way to play this is to divide the group into pairs and give each person six clothespins. Each person then tries to hang all his pins on his partner. The winners then pair off again, and so on until there is a champion clothespinner.

CRAB BALL

This is an active game for groups of twenty or more. All that is needed is a playground ball. Divide into four teams of equal size, and form a square with each team forming one side of the square. Players should then sit down on the floor, and number off from one to however many players are on each team. To begin the game the leader places the ball in the center and calls a number. All four persons of that number "crab walk" out to the ball. "Crab Walking" is bending over backwards and then walking on all fours. The object is to kick the ball over the heads of one of the other teams (other than one's own). When a crab walker succeeds in kicking it over

24

the heads of another team, the team over whose head it went, gets a point. The remaining members of the team must stay in place with their seats on the floor. They may block the balls coming at them either by kicking, using their bodies, or using their heads. They may never use their hands or arms. They also may try to kick it over the heads of an opposing team. Either way the team over whose head the ball goes gets the point. When the first team reaches ten points, the game is ended and the *lowest* score wins.

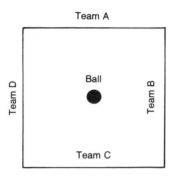

CROWS AND CRANES

Divide the group into two teams. One side is the "Crows," the other is the "Cranes." The two teams are lined up facing each other on two lines four or five feet apart. The leader flips a coin (heads—"Crows," tails—"Cranes") and yells out the name of the team which won the toss. If he yells "Crows," the "Crows" must turn around and run, with the "Cranes" in hot pursuit. If any of the "Cranes" succeed in touching a member (or members) of the "Crows" before he crosses a given line (20 to 60 feet away), he is considered a captive of the "Cranes" and must aid the "Cranes" when play continues. The team which captures all the members of the other team is the winner.

DOMINO

This is a great game for larger groups that is not only fun to play, but fun to watch as well. It's also easy to play and requires no props. Teams line up in single file lines with teams parallel to each other. There should be the same number of people (exactly) in each line, and everyone should face the same direction, toward the front of the line. On a signal (whistle, etc.), the first person in each line squats, then the next person (behind him) also squats, then the next person and so on all the way down to the end of the team's line. (You cannot squat down until the person immediately in front of you squats first.) The last person in line squats and then quickly stands back up again, and the whole process repeats itself, only in reverse, with each person standing up in succession instead of squatting. (Again, you cannot stand up until the person *behind* you first stands up.) The team which completes this first, with the person at the front of the line standing, is the winner.

The effect of this visually is much like standing "dominoes" up side by side and pushing over the one on the end toward the others. Each domino falls in succession to the end of the line. This game is much like that, only the "dominoes" first go down, then back up again. It works best with at least 25 or so in each line (the more the better). Have the group try it several times for speed.

ELASTIC BAND RELAY

In preparation for this game, cut a strip of inch wide elastic 36 inches long. Overlap one inch and stitch on a sewing machine. The result will be a large elastic circle.

Break group into teams of eight to twelve players. Supply each team with an elastic band. At the starting signal, the first player brings the band over his head and body before passing it on to the next player on the team. The first team to have all the players pass the elastic band over their bodies is the winning team.

Variations may have the players passing the elastic band up from the feet, or couples passing the band over both bodies at once.

FEET ON THE ROCKS

Divide your group into two teams. Have each team sit back to back with an approximate five foot space between the chairs. The captain of each team sits in a separate chair at the end of the team row of chairs.

At the signal, an ice cube is placed under one of the feet of each captain. The captains slide the ice to player Number One on their team. Player Number One must pass it from one foot to the other and then to the next player on the team. This continues until the ice cube is passed by the entire team back to the captain again. The captain is now allowed to stand up and devise a way to carry the ice cube with his or her feet only to the opposite end of the room and put it into a cup (no hands).

If the captain drops the ice cube, he or she can start from where it was dropped, but if the ice cube melts or slips out of reach while the team is passing it, they must start over again.

FLAMINGO VOLLEYBALL

Here's a guys vs. gals game that can really be a lot of fun. Announce to your group a volleyball game between the girls and the guys. After the teams are selected and ready to play, give the guys one additional instruction that you supposedly forgot to mention. The rules are the same as regular volleyball except that when the ball is in play, every guy must hold one ankle. Failure to do so results in a point for the other team.

FLY SWATTER

This is a good little game taken from "Pin the Tail on the Donkey." Blindfold a kid, give him a fly swatter (the type with holes in it) and spin him around a few times. Place a glob of shaving cream on the wall and have the kid try to swat it. On impact the "swatter" usually gets hit with flying shaving cream. Wipe it up and position a new glob in a different spot for the next contestant. The winner is whoever can swat the glob in the fastest time.

FOUR TEAM DODGEBALL

This is a fast moving game that is best played in a gym or similar room. Divide the group into four teams of equal size. If you have a basketball court marked on the floor, this can be used as the playing area, otherwise you will need to mark off your own boundaries with tape or some other method. The floor is divided into quadrants similar to the diagram below:

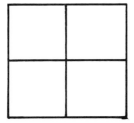

Each team is assigned one of the four areas and team members cannot leave their assigned area during the game. A volleyball, beachball, or playground ball should be used (not as hard or as large as a basketball). The rules are basically the same as regular dodgeball, except that a player may throw the ball at anyone in any of the other three quadrants. If a player is hit below the belt with the ball, he or she is out of the game. If the ball misses and goes out of bounds, the referee tosses the ball into the team that was thrown at (where it went out of bounds). If a player is thrown at and catches the ball before it hits the floor, without dropping it, the player that threw it is out. The winning team is the team that lasts the longest (the team that still has at least one player after the other teams have been eliminated), or the team with the most players left at the end of a specified time limit.

FRISBEE RELAY

Divide the group into equally sized teams of 5 or 6 per team. Any number of teams can play at once. Each team will need a frisbee. The playing area should have plenty of length, such as a road (without traffic) or a large open field. Each team should spread out in a line with players about 50 feet apart or so. The first person throws the frisbee to the second, who allows the frisbee to land. That person then stands where the frisbee landed and throws it towards the third person, who throws it to the fourth, and so on. The object is to see which team can throw it the greatest distance in the shortest time. Award points for throwing it the farthest, and points for finishing first. For added fun, have the guys throw left-handed (or right-handed if they are left-handed). Footballs can be substituted for frisbees if they are easier to get.

HAND-IN-GLOVE RELAY

This is a relay game in which the teams stand in line and pass a pair of gloves from one end to the other. The first person puts the gloves on, then the next person takes them off and puts them on himself. Each person takes the gloves off the person in front of him and puts them on himself. All fingers of the hand must fit in the fingers of the gloves. Options: Use rubber kitchen gloves or large work gloves.

HAPPY HANDFUL RELAY

This relay can be easily adapted for indoor or outdoor use. Assemble two identical sets of at least 12 miscellaneous items (i.e., 2 brooms, 2 balls, 2 skillets, 2 rolls of bathroom tissue, 2 ladders, etc.). Use your imagination to collect an interesting variety of identical pairs of objects. Place the two sets of objects on two separate tables.

Line up a team for each table. The first player for each team runs to his table, picks up one item of his choice, runs back to his team and passes the item to the second player. The second player carries the first item back to the table, picks up another item and carries both items back to the third player. Each succeeding player carries the items collected by his teammates to the table, picks up one new item and carries them all back to the next player. The game will begin rapidly, but the pace will slow as each player decides which item to add to a growing armload of items. It will also take increasingly longer for one player to pass his burden to the next player in line.

Once picked up, an item cannot touch the table or floor. Any item which is dropped in transit or transfer must be returned to the table by the leader. No one may assist the giving and receiving players in the exchange of items except through coaching. The first team to empty its table wins.

HIP CHARADES

This is a great game for casual get-togethers. It is played just like charades, except that team members spell out words with their *hips* instead of using pantomine or hand signals. Each contestant tries to get his team to guess the words he is spelling out by standing with his *back* to the team and moving his hips to form (or "write") the letters in the air. The team shouts out each letter as they recognize it and attempt to guess the correct title in the fastest time possible. The results are hilarious.

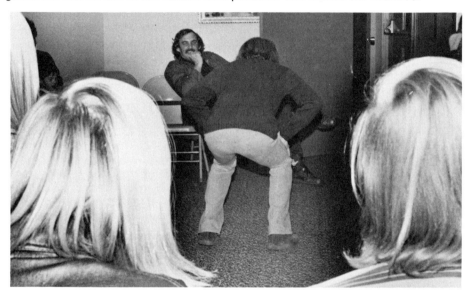

HULA HOOPLA

The "hula-hoop" will never die. It has been around for quite a few years and should be around quite a few more. In light of this incredible truth, here are a few "hula-hoop relays" that can be a lot of fun. Divide into teams and run these relays in normal relay fashion. Each team should have a hula-hoop.

1. Place a hula-hoop on the floor 20 feet or so in front of each team. The object is for each player to run to the hoop, pick it up, and "hula" it around five or ten times (you decide how many), drop it to the floor and return to the line.

29

2. The object of this relay is for each person to take a hula-hoop and "hula" it while walking or running to a certain point 20 feet or so from the team and back. If the hula-hoop drops, the player must stop, get the hoop going again, and continue.

3. Place the hoop 20 feet or so away from the team once again. This time the player must run to the hoop and try to pass it over his body without using his hands. In other words, he must stand in the hoop and work it up and over his head with just his feet, legs, arms, etc., but no hands.

4. This relay is similar to the one above only two or three people run to the hoop at the same time, and without hands work the hoop up around their waists. They then run to a point and back with the hoop in place around their waists. At no time may their hands be used to hold the hoop up.

MAD RELAY

This is a different kind of relay race in which each contestant does something different. What the contestants do is determined by the directions in a bag at the other end of the relay course.

At the beginning of the race, each team is lined up single file as usual. On a signal, the first person on each team runs to the other end of the course to a chair. On the chair ís a bag containing instructions written on separate pieces of paper. The contestant draws one of the instructions, reads it, and follows it as quickly as possible. Before returning to the team, the contestant must tag the chair. The contestant then runs back and tags the next runner. The relay proceeds in this manner and the team that uses all of its instructions first is the winner. Below are a few sample directions:

1. Run around the chair 5 times while continuously yelling, "The British are coming, the British are coming."
2. Run to the nearest person on another team and scratch his head.
3. Run to the nearest adult in the room and whisper, "You're no spring chicken."
4. Stand on one foot while holding the other in your hand, tilt your head back and count, "10, 9, 8, 7, 6, 5, 4, 3, 2, 1, Blast off!"
5. Take your shoes off, put them on the wrong feet, and then tag your nearest opponent.
6. Sit on the floor, cross your legs, and sing the following: "Mary had a little lamb, little lamb, little lamb, Mary had a little lamb, its fleece was white as snow."
7. Go to the last person on your team and make 3 different "funny-face" expressions, then return to the chair before tagging your next runner.
8. Put your hands over your eyes, snort like a pig 5 times, meow like a cat 5 times.
9. Sit in the chair, fold your arms, and laugh hard and loud for 5 seconds.
10. Run around the chair backwards 5 times while clapping your hands.

11. Go to a blond-headed person and keep asking, "Do blonds really have more fun?", until he or she answers.
12. Run to someone not on your team and kiss his hand and gently pinch his cheek.

MAGAZINE SCAVENGER HUNT

Divide your group into teams of two or three persons each and give each group a combination of old magazines. Then give them a list of various items, photos, names, etc., that could be found in the magazines. As soon as a group finds one of the items, they cut it out and collect as many as they can in the time limit. The list can be long or short depending on the time. Some of the items will be found in several magazines while others in only one. You can make the list as difficult as you want. The winner, of course, is the team with the most items found.

MATCH UP

This is a variation of the old television game show "The Match Game." Divide into two or more teams of equal number. Have each team choose a team captain who goes to the front of the room with the other team captain(s). Everyone, including the team captains, should have several sheets of paper and pencils.

The leader then asks the entire group a question, such as "Who is going to win the World Series this year?" Everyone, without any discussion, writes his or her answer down on one slip of paper, and passes it in to the team captain, who has also written down an answer. When ready, the team captains announce their answers, and a point is awarded to each team for every answer from that team which matches their team captain's. In other words, if the team captain answered, "The Dodgers," then his or her team would get a point for every other answer from that team which also was "The Dodgers."

Some sample questions: *(Make up your own.)*
1. If you were going to repaint this room, what color would you do it in?
2. What country in the world would you most like to visit?
3. Your favorite T.V. show?
4. A number between one and five?
5. What book of the Bible has the most to say about good works?
6. What's the best way to have fun in this town?
7. What's the funniest word you can think of?
8. How many children do you think you will have in your life?

MATH SCRAMBLE

Divide into teams. Each person is given a number on a piece of paper which is to be worn. (Numbers should begin at 0 and go up to 10 or the number of kids on the team.) The leader stands an equal distance away from each team and yells out a "math problem" such as "2 times 8 minus 4 divided by 3" and the team must send the person with the correct answer (the person wearing the number "4" in this case) to the leader. No talking is allowed on the team. The correct person must simply get up and run. The first correct answer to get to the leader wins 100 points. The first team to reach 1,000 (or whatever) wins.

MUDDY MARBLE SCRAMBLE

Here's a wild game for hot weather and large groups. Churn up a mud hole (figure approximately 1 or 2 square feet per kid). Then work hundreds of different colored marbles into the top 5 or 6 inches of mud. (Make sure the mud is without too many rocks.) Each different colored marble is worth a different amount of points. The fewer you have of one color, the more points they are worth. For example:

1 red marble: 500 points
2 white marbles: 100 points each
25 blue marbles: 50 points each
100 green marbles: 20 points each

Divide the group up into teams, each with two leaders—one who washes off the recovered marbles, the other keeps track of how many of each color have been recovered. At the signal, all of the participants dive in the mud and search for marbles for 10-15 minutes. When time is called, the team with the most points wins.

NERF FOOTBALL LEAGUE

Now your youth group can have its very own "N.F.L." This crazy version of football can be played indoors with almost any number of kids. You could divide into teams and have a "Nerf Football Tournament," with the Super Bowl as its climax. Here's the way the game is played.

1. Basic football rules are in force. The object is to score touchdowns. Your football field should be marked with boundaries, goal lines, etc.
2. There is absolutely no running or fast walking allowed. The "officials" can determine penalties for this. All players must walk when the ball is in play.
3. There are only four downs allowed. No first downs. If you can't score a TD in four, then the ball is turned over to the other team.
4. Passing can be in any direction to any player on your team. There can be more than one pass per down. In other words, players can keep passing the ball until someone is finally tagged by an opposing player.

5. No tackling. This should be two-hand touch anywhere, or "flag" football.
6. Don't replay "interference" calls. Low ceilings, furniture, etc., are all part of the game. Adapt the rules to whatever environment you have.
7. The ball must be a soft, spongy "Nerf" ball (available in any toy store) or something similar.

NERFKETBALL

Here is a fun version of basketball using a "nerf" ball (soft sponge) and chairs. Choose two teams of equal numbers and seat them alternately on sturdy chairs as shown in the diagram: two rows of players facing each other. For best results, players should be spaced at least double arm's distance apart both sideways and across. Place a "basket" (small bucket, gallon plastic bottle with top cut off, etc.) at each end of the double row, approximately six feet from the players at the ends of the rows. The basket should also be on the floor.

The two basic ground rules of the game are: (1) Chairs cannot be moved or tipped; (2) Each player must remain seated while the ball is in play.

Using a coin flip, one team is chosen to take first possession of the ball. Play begins as the player farthest from his team's goal is given the ball by the referee. The team tries to work the ball toward their goal by passing it while opponents try to block passes and steal the ball. Any player may take a shot at the goal at any time, but the advantages of passing the ball to the player nearest the goal are obvious. If the ball is intercepted by the other team, play continues in the opposite direction.

When an attempted field goal misses, the ball is automatically "out" to the other team and play then goes the other way. When a field goal is scored, all players rotate one seat to the right. This will give each player the opportunity to be his team's prime shooter during the game. After rotation, the ball goes "out" to the other team and goes the other way.

Any ball loose within the playing area is a free ball. Any ball going outside the playing area is given to the player nearest the last player to touch the ball.

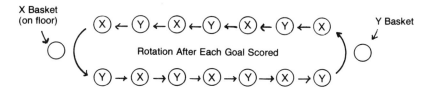

Penalties may be assessed and free throws awarded for players leaving their seats or for unnecessary roughness. Limit the game by using a kitchen timer for quarters or halves, or by setting a scoring limit.

NEW VOLLEYBALL

Here is a great new way to play the old game of volleyball. "New Volleyball" can be played on a regular volleyball court, with the normal amount of players on each team. A regular volleyball is used as well. The main difference is the scoring.

The object of the game is for a team to volley the ball as many times as possible without missing or fouling (up to 20 times) before hitting it back over the net to the opposing team who will make every attempt to return it without missing. If they do miss, the opposite team receives as many points as they volleyed before sending it over the net. All volleys must be counted audibly by the entire team (or by scorers on the sidelines) which aids in the scoring process and also helps build tension. So the idea is to volley the ball as many times as possible each time the ball comes over the net and hope that the other team blows it.

Other rules:

1. No person may hit the ball two consecutive times.
2. No two people may hit the ball back and forth to each other more than once in succession to increase the number of volleys. In other words, player A may hit it to player B, but player B may not hit it back to player A. Player A may hit it again once someone else has hit it besides player B.
3. Five points are awarded to the serving team if the opposing team fails to return a serve.
4. Five points are awarded to the receiving team if a serve is missed (out-of-bounds, in the net, etc.)
5. Players rotate on each serve, even if the serving team scores on successive serves.
6. A game is fifteen minutes. The highest score wins.
7. All other volleyball rules are in effect.

PAGE SCRAMBLE

Give each team a children's story book with titles such as "Waldo the Jumping Dragon" or "Big Albert Moves into Town." The dumber the better. You must also make sure each book has the same number of pages. Before passing them out, however, carefully remove the pages from each book cover, and mix them up so that each team has a book with the correct number of pages . . . but not the correct pages. On a signal, the teams distribute the pages among team members and they begin trading page for page with other teams. The whole place becomes a giant trading floor. The first team with a completed book, with pages in the correct order, wins.

PAPER SHOOT

Divide into teams of from four to eight kids each. Set a garbage can up in the middle of the room (about three feet high), and prepare ahead of time several paper batons and a lot of wadded up paper balls. One team lies down around the trash can with their heads toward the can (on their backs). Each of these players has a paper baton. The opposing team stands around the trash can behind a line about ten feet or so away from the can. This line can be a large circle drawn around the can. The opposing team tries to throw wadded up paper balls into the can, and the defending team tries to knock the balls away with their paper batons while lying on their backs. The opposing team gets two minutes to try and shoot as much paper into the can as possible. After each team has had its chance to be in both positions, the team that got the most paper balls into the can is declared the winner. To make the game a bit more difficult for the throwers, have them sit in chairs while they toss the paper.

PINCH ME

Here's a wild game that is great for dividing a large group into smaller groups. Everyone is to remain silent (no talking, but laughing, screaming, etc. is permitted). Each person receives a slip of paper which he is to keep secret from everyone else. The papers all read something like:

Pinch Me	Step on My Toes
Slap Me	Rub My Tummy
Tickle Me	Scratch My Back
Pull My Ear	

When everyone has a card, the leader yells "go" and the players must find the others in their group. For instance, a "Pinch Me" must go around pinching everyone until he finds someone else who is a "Pinch Me." They stick together pinching others until they find the rest of their team. There should be an equal number of each group. After a period of time, the leader stops the game, and the team that has done the best job of getting together wins.

PING PONG BALL FLOAT

For this relay, you will need coffee cans (empty), ping pong balls, buckets of water, towels, and one guy with his shirt off for every team participating.

The guy with his shirt off lies on his back about ten yards from his team who are in a single-file line. Place the coffee can (empty) on his stomach or chest. Put the ping pong ball in the coffee can. A bucket full of water goes beside each team.

As the game begins, players use their cupped hands to carry water from their buckets to the coffee cans. Each player goes one at a time. As the coffee can fills with water, the ping pong ball rises in the can. As soon as it is high enough, a player tries to remove it from the can with his mouth. The first team to get the ping pong ball out of the can (no hands) and back across the finish line, wins.

PYRAMID CLUMPS

This game is very similar to "Clumps" with a fun little twist. Have your kids mill around the floor. Then the leader blows the whistle or horn and yells out any number. After the number is called, the participants seek out the called number of kids, get down on their hands and knees and build a "pyramid." The pyramid group must have exactly the called number of kids or they are out of the game. Extra people are also out. The game continues until one individual or one small group remains.

SHUFFLE YOUR BUNS

Arrange chairs in a circle so that everyone has a chair. There should be two extra chairs in the circle. Each person sits in a chair except for two people in the middle who try to sit in the two vacant chairs. The persons sitting in the chairs keep moving

36

around from chair to chair to prevent the two in the middle from sitting down. If one or both of the two in the middle manage to sit in a chair, the person on his right replaces him in the middle of the circle and then tries to sit in an empty chair.

SILLY SOCCER

Divide your group into two teams. In a large open field, place two pylons 100 to 150 feet apart. The object is to hit the opposing team's pylon with the ball. There are no boundaries, and the pylon may be hit from any direction. All other soccer rules apply. For added confusion with a large group, throw in a second ball.

SQUAT

This game can really be fun, and if everything is not done quite right, it can be a spectacular flop. First of all, get everyone in a circle shoulder to shoulder. Then have everyone turn right, facing the back of the person in front of him. On the count of three, sit down.

If everything is done right, everyone will simultaneously sit down on the lap of the person behind him. If the timing isn't quite right . . . well. To make the game even more precarious, have everyone cross his right leg over his left before sitting down. Make sure everyone's hands are out to the side.

STACK 'EM UP

Have everyone sit in chairs in a circle. Prepare a list of qualifying characteristics such as these few examples:

1. If you forgot to use a deodorant today . . .
2. If you got a traffic ticket this year . . .
3. If you have a hole in your sock . . .
4. If you are afraid of the dark . . .

Then read them one at a time and add ". . . move three chairs to the right" or "move one chair to the left," etc. In other words, you might say, "If you forgot to use a deodorant today, *move three chairs to the right,* and all those who "qualify" move as instructed and sit in that chair, regardless of whether or not it's occupied by one or more persons. As the game progresses, kids begin "stacking up" on certain chairs.

THROUGH THE LEGS SUFFLE

Here's the old "through-the-legs" game with a new twist. Have the teams line up single file spreading their legs apart enough so that someone can crawl through them. Everyone must have his hands on the hips of the person in front of them. The lines must be behind the starting line. On the signal, the last person crawls through the legs of the team and stands up at the front of the line. As soon as he stands up, the person who is now at the rear of the line crawls through, etc. The line moves forward and the first team to cross the goal line wins. Only one person per team can be crawling at a time.

TUG-O-WAR IN THE ROUND

Get a large rope about 24 feet in length and tie (or splice) the two ends together, making one round rope. In the center of a square, the rope is placed opened out into a circle. Four teams line up on four sides of the square. The teams should be equal in size and each team should number off from one on up. The leader then calls out a number and the four kids (one from each team) with that number grab one side of the rope and try to get back across their teams's line. As soon as a player crosses the line (pulling the rope), he is declared the winner. Continue until everyone has had a try.

WATER BALLOON VOLLEYBALL

Water Balloon Volleyball is played very similarly to a regular game of conventional volleyball. Set up your volleyball net as usual, and divide the young people into equal sides. This type of volleyball is not restricted to the conventional 6-member, 9-member team, but any number of young people may play. Of course, the main difference in this game is that instead of using a regular volleyball, you use a water balloon for the ball. The service takes place from the back line and each team is allowed three tosses and three catches in order to get the water balloon over the net to the opposing team. The opposing team then has three tosses and three catches in order to get the ball back across the net. The balloon is continually tossed back and forth across the net until, finally, breakage occurs. When the balloon breaks, the side on which it breaks does not score, but rather, the opposite team gets the point, without regard to who did the serving. Spikes are allowed, but again, if the balloon breaks on the team who is doing the spiking, the other team is awarded the point. The team that then wins the point, regardless of which team it is, is the team that continues to serve until service is broken. The game is played to a regular volleyball score of 15, at which time sides of the net are changed and the game resumes. All other rules in regular volleyball are in effect for this game, such as out-of-bound lines, not being able to cross over the net with your hand, or falling into the net with your body.

Another variation of this game which proves to be even more fun, is to include up to 30 or 40 members on each team and insert into play 4 or 5 water balloons, so that there are several opportunities for returns, spikes, and services all at the same time. The rules for this game are the same as for the one-ball system. There is no official scoring for this game. The winning team is simply the driest team at the end of an allotted period of time.

3 | Creative Communication

BACK RUBS AND THE GOSPEL

Here is a fun way to help people to experience touching and community in a safe and non-threatening atmosphere. (It feels good, too.) Each person is to give or to receive back rubs according to the following list which should be printed up so that everyone has a copy. Following the "back rubbing" period (twenty minutes or so), follow up with a discussion. Some discussion questions are provided.

Rules:

1. You may not receive two back rubs in a row.
2. The *giver* will be scored by the *receiver* on a scale of 1 to 10 with 10 being the best.
3. On your sheet, the score is automatically 5 points for any back rub *received* by you.
4. You will receive a score from 1 to 10 only on back rubs which you give. The receiver will judge your back rub.
5. No score is valid without the initials of the other person (giver or receiver).
6. You may not refuse to give or receive a back rub if someone asks you.
7. The same person may be used only twice, once giving and once receiving.
8. The highest score at the end of the time limit wins.

Questions for Discussion:

1. What are some feelings you had? Were you embarrassed? How did you feel if you could only give? Or only get?
2. Those who did both, did you like giving or receiving better?

3. Has this experience affected your feelings in any way with the rest of the group?
4. Are there any insights to be gained from this about Christian love?

The Back Rubs:	Score	Initial
1. Give to some one taller.		
2. Receive from someone shorter.		
3. Give to someone older.		
4. Receive from someone younger.		
5. Give to someone of the opposite sex.		
6. Receive from someone of the same sex.		
7. Give to someone with shoes on.		
8. Receive from someone without shoes on.		
9. Give to someone with blue eyes.		
10. Receive from someone with brown eyes.		
11. Give to someone wearing red.		
12. Receive from someone wearing green.		
13. Give to someone who lives less than one mile from you.		
14. Receive from someone who lives more than one mile from you.		
15. Give to someone who wears glasses or contacts.		
16. Receive from someone who doesn't wear glasses or contacts.		
17. Give to someone with an even numbered address.		
18. Receive from someone with an even address.		
19. Give to someone whose last initial is before yours in the alphabet.		
20. Receive from someone whose last initial is after yours in the alphabet.		

CARE COMPANY

This idea is designed to help bring about greater fellowship or *Koinonia* among members of the group. Begin with a 15 minute discussion of what "cliques" are and how they differ from "interest groups," etc. Then appropriate scripture can be read. (Romans 12:3-16, 1 Corinthians 1:11-13 and 12:12-27.) Following the reading of Scripture, groups of five are then formed (at random) and each person gives his name, age, school, etc., and shares two things he likes, and two things he dislikes. After all are through, a new group of five is formed and the same procedure is followed. At the conclusion of the meeting each person finds someone he doesn't normally associate with and after sharing the same information, close with a prayer for each other.

At the next meeting a "Care Package" is given to each person. It is simply a card or sheet of paper listing five persons (including themselves), chosen at random, who are members of their "care company." Also on the sheet or card is a "pledge," which each person is asked to accept and carry out as best they can:

I PLEDGE TO:
1. Call or contact the members of my "care company" at least once a week just to see how things are going.
2. Make a personal effort to get to know them as well as possible.
3. Meet new people and expand my "care company" to at least ten by (date) _____.
4. To pray for each member of my "care company" every day.

This can be an annual thing, and kids should be encouraged to keep it up all year long, and report how things are going with their "care company" on a regular basis.

CHRISTMAS I.Q. TEST

Next Christmas, give the following "quiz" to your youth, to determine how much they *really* know about the Bible's most popular story. The results will undoubtedly be very embarrassing as well as lead to a better understanding of the events surrounding Christs' birth.

Instructions:

Read and answer each question in the order it appears. When choices are given, read them carefully and select the best one. Put a "T" or an "F" in the blank on all True or False questions. Guessing is permitted, cheating is not . . .

_____ 1. As long as Christmas has been celebrated, it has been on December 25th. *(True or False)*

_____ 2. Joseph was from:
   A. Bethlehem
   B. Jerusalem
   C. Nazareth
   D. Egypt
   E. Minnesota
   F. None of the above

_____ 3. How did Mary and Joseph travel to Bethlehem?
   A. Camel
   B. Donkey
   C. Walked
   D. Volkswagen
   E. Joseph walked, Mary rode a donkey
   F. Who knows?

_____ 4. Mary and Joseph were married when Mary became pregnant. *(True or False)*

_____ 5. Mary and Joseph were married when Jesus was born. *(True or False)*

43

6. What did the innkeeper tell Mary and Joseph?
   A. "Come back after the Christmas
      rush and I should have some
      vacancies."
   B. "I have a stable you can use."
   C. "There is no room in the inn."
   D. Both B and C
   E. None of the above

7. Jesus was delivered in a:
   A. Stable
   B. Manger
   C. Cave
   D. Barn
   E. Unknown

8. A "manger" is a:
   A. Stable for domestic animals
   B. Wooden hay storage bin
   C. Feeding trough
   D. Barn

9. Which animals does the Bible say were present at Jesus' birth?
   A. Cows, sheep, goats
   B. Cows, donkeys, sheep
   C. Sheep and goats only
   D. Miscellaneous barnyard
      animals
   E. Lions, tigers, elephants
   F. None of the above

10. Who saw the "star in the east"?
    A. Shepherds
    B. Mary and Joseph
    C. Three Kings
    D. Both A and C
    E. None of the above

11. How many angels spoke to the shepherds?
    A. One
    B. Three
    C. A "Multitude"
    D. None of the above

12. What "sign" did the angels tell the shepherds to look for?
    A. "This way to baby Jesus "
    B. A star over Bethlehem
    C. A baby that doesn't cry
    D. A house with a
       Christmas tree
    E. A baby in a stable
    F. None of the above

13. What did the angels sing?
    A. "Joy to the World, the Lord is Come"
    B. "Alleluia"
    C. "Unto us a child is born,
       unto us a son is given"
    D. "Glory to God in the
       highest, etc."
    E. "Glory to the Newborn King"
    F. "My Sweet Lord"

14. What is a "Heavenly Host"?
    A. Angel at the gate of heaven
    B. Angel who invites people to heaven
    C. Angel who serves refreshments
       in heaven
    D. An angel choir
    E. An angel army
    F. None of the above

15. There was snow that first Christmas:
    A. Only in Bethlehem.
    B. All over Israel.
    C. Nowhere in Israel.
    D. Somewhere in Israel.
    E. Mary and Joseph only "dreamed" of a white Christmas.

16. The baby Jesus cried:
    A. When the doctor slapped him on his behind.
    B. Just like other babies cry.
    C. When the little drummer boy started banging on his drum.
    D. He never cried.

17. What is "frankincense"?
    A. A precious metal.
    B. A precious fabric.
    C. A precious perfume.
    D. An eastern monster story.
    E. None of the above.

18. What is "myrrh"?
    A. An easily shaped metal.
    B. A spice used for burying people.
    C. A drink.
    D. After-shave lotion.
    E. None of the above.

19. How many wise men came to see Jesus?
    (Write in the correct number.)

20. What does "wise men" refer to?
    A. Men of the educated class.
    B. They were eastern Kings.
    C. They were astrologers.
    D. They were smart enough to follow the star.
    E. They were "sages."

21. The wise men found Jesus in a:
    A. Manger
    B. Stable
    C. House
    D. Holiday Inn
    E. Good Mood

22. The wise men stopped in Jerusalem:
    A. To inform Herod about Jesus.
    B. To find out where Jesus was.
    C. To ask about the star they saw.
    D. For gas.
    E. To buy presents for Jesus.

23. Where do we find the Christmas story in order to check up on all these ridiculous questions?
    A. Matthew
    B. Mark
    C. Luke
    D. John
    E. All of the above.
    F. Only A and B
    G. Only A and C
    H. Only A, B and C
    I. Only X, Y and Z
    J. Aesops Fables

_____ 24. When Joseph and Mary found out that Mary was pregnant with Jesus, what happened?

A. They got married.
B. Joseph wanted to break the engagement.
C. Mary left town for three months.
D. An angel told them to go to Bethlehem.
E. Both A and D
F. Both B and C

_____ 25. Who told Mary and Joseph to go to Bethlehem?

A. The angel.
B. Mary's mother.
C. Herod.
D. Caesar Augustus.
E. Alexander the Great.
F. No one told them to.

_____ 26. Joseph took the baby Jesus to Egypt:

A. To show him the pyramids.
B. To teach him the wisdom of the pharoahs.
C. To put him in a basket in the reeds by the river.
D. Because he dreamed about it.
E. To be taxed.
F. Joseph did not take Jesus to Egypt.
G. None of the above.

_____ 27. I think that this test was:

A. Super
B. Great
C. Fantastic
D. All of the above.

Answers:

1. False. Not until the 4th Century did it settle on the 25th. Other dates were accepted before then.
2. A. See Luke 2:3, 4.
3. F. The Bible doesn't say.
4. False. See Matthew 1:18.
5. False. See Luke 2:5.
6. E. No word about the innkeeper. See Luke 2:7.
7. E. No word about it. See Luke 2:7.
8. C.
9. F. The Bible doesn't specify.
10. E. The _wise men_ did (they were not Kings). See Matthew 2:2.
11. A. See Luke 2:9.
12. F. See Luke 2:12.
13. D. See Luke 2:14.
14. E. Definition is an "army." See _Living Bible_ also.
15. D. Mt. Hermon is snow covered.
16. C. We have no reason to believe he wouldn't.
17. B. By definition.
18. B. See John 19:39 or a dictionary.
19. No one knows. See Matthew 2:1.
20. C. See most any commentary. They were astrologers or "star gazers."
21. C. See Matthew 2:11.
22. B. See Matthew 2:1-20.
23. G. Mark begins with John the Baptist, John with "the word."
24. F. See Matthew 1:19, Luke 1:39, 56.
25. D. See Luke 2:1, 4.
26. D. See Matthew 2:13.
27. D, of course.

DEAR ABBY

Occasionally young people encounter situations in which they would like advice in a Christian atmosphere, but are embarrassed about bringing their questions openly before their peers. This suggestion might provide an answer to the problem.

Give each young person a piece of paper and a pencil and instruct him to write down in letter form, some problem that is bothering him. This could be a family problem, a problem at school, a problem that requires Christian advice. The letter should be addressed to "Dear Abby" to give the feeling of appealing to some uninvolved source. These would be signed with an anonymous signature ("Concerned" or "Wants to Know"). The letters would then be collected and read to the group for their advice.

This not only gives the group a chance to help (who knows, their advice might be better than an adult's), but also gives them a chance to see that others are having problems very similar to their own.

ENGLISH TEST

Below is a fun way to show kids how we often make judgments too hastily. Pass out copies of the following paragraph and have each person make the corrections as instructed. Most will blow it every time. When they are finished, follow up with a discussion on Matthew 7:1-6.

Mark this paragraph into sentences using capitals at the beginning, periods at the end of sentences, and commas, etc. where needed. Once begun, DO NOT GO BACK and try to correct.

He is a young man yet experienced in vice and wickedness he is never found in opposing the works of iniquity he takes delight in the downfall of his neighbors he never rejoices in the prosperity of his fellow-creatures he is always ready to assist in destroying the peace of society he takes no pleasure in serving the Lord he is uncommonly diligent in sowing discord among his friends and acquaintances he takes no pride in laboring to promote the cause of Christianity he has not been negligent in endeavoring to tear down the church he makes no effort to subdue his evil passions he strives hard to build up Satan's kingdom he lends no aid to the support of the gospel among heathen he contributes largely to the devil he will never go to heaven he must go where he will receive his just reward.

Here is the way it should be corrected.

He is a young man, yet experienced. In vice and wickedness, he is never found. In opposing the works of iniquity, he takes delight. In the downfall of his neighbors, he never rejoices. In destroying the peace of society, he takes no pleasure. In serving the Lord, he is uncommonly diligent. In sowing discord among his friends and acquaintances, he takes no pride. In laboring to promote the cause of Christianity, he has not been negligent. In endeavoring to tear down the church, he makes no effort. To subdue his evil passions, he strives hard. To build up Satan's kingdom, he lends no aid. To the support of the gospel among heathen, he contributes largely. To the devil he will never go. To heaven he must go, where he will receive his just reward.

ESTHER AND THE KING

The Old Testament book of Esther is one of the most fascinating stories of the Bible and is an excellent book for group study and discussion.

Have the group read through the entire book in one sitting. This normally takes about 20 minutes (if you read from a modern translation). Then discuss these questions:

1. Esther never mentions the name of God. In spite of this, can you find evidence of God in Esther? (Have the group take a chapter at a time and point out places where they find God, such as verses 4:14 or 6:1-2. There are many more.)

2. Discuss the *advice* that was given to various people in the story. (Such as 1:16, 3:8, 4:13, 5:14, etc.) Which was good advice, which was bad? Who gives *you* advice?

3. Rank order the main characters in the story from best to worst. Who was the best person, who was the worst? (Give reasons why.) The main characters are (in alphabetical order):

   a. Ahasuerus, the King
   b. Esther
   c. Haman
   d. Memucan (1:16)
   e. Mordecai
   f. Vashti, the Queen
   g. Zeresh, Haman's wife

4. If you could write a "moral to the story," what would it be?

Of course, there are other excellent questions that will come up in the study of Esther, but these will help towards good discussion.

Esther can also be written as a play and acted out for the church very effectively. The story contains interesting dialogue and characters, a good plot, suspense, and a bit of irony. Most of all it will help young people to gain more insights into and appreciation for the Old Testament.

THE EXECUTION

The following short play is good for use as a discussion starter or as a statement on the meaning of the Crucifixion. It requires two characters who have speaking parts

(Calvinicus and Georgius) and any number of others who carry out the action as described in the column "Visual" below. Calvinicus and Georgius carry on their conversation totally oblivious to what is going on behind them.

VISUAL	AUDIO
Camera (or spotlight) on men eating lunch.	*Calvinicus:* Hi, George, What's new?
	Georgius: What d'ya mean? Nothing ever happens around here. Looks like another hot one. Nice day for camels, eh?
	C: (chuckles) Yeah, pass me an olive, will ya?
	G: Here you are, ya beggar. Why don't you get yourself a bowl and sit at the Jerusalem gate?
	C: Lay off, ok? It's been rough enough today out there in the fields. Look at these fingernails!
People start walking across behind the workmen.	G: Yeah, I know. The ground is so hard. Almost broke the yoke right off my ox.
	C: What's going on anyway? What's all this commotion about?
	G: Oh, just another execution. You know, one of those weird "prophets." Claim they got the answer to all the world's problems. Bein' executed along with two other criminals.
	C: Oh. He's the guy. Yeah, I heard about him. They say he's God or something. Some people say he did some kind of hocus pocus on some sick people.
	G: Yeah. These "prophets" are all the same. They supposedly fix a few legs and eyes and everyone goes ga-ga.
A small cross is carried in and set to one side.	Course, he's also charged with creating a disturbance, inciting a riot, and contempt of court. They never learn. If he really wants a following, he's gotta explain how come his God is so good at fixing legs and so bad at gettin' him outta jail. Uh . . . look . . . I gotta get back to the house and start preparing for the feast tonight.
	C: You know, George, just the other day I was telling the wife what a mess the world is in. On one hand you got those radical Zealots and Essenes walking around with the short hair and stuff, and on the other hand you got those phony loudmouthed Pharisees running around blowing trumpets and prayin' in your ear. What are things coming to anyway?

G: I don't know, man. Why don't you ask Caesar?

C: I know this sounds weird, George, but sometimes I think if there is a God, I wish he'd do something radical about what's goin' on down here. I mean, you know, he could always come down here and zap a few Romans. Then maybe something would happen.

A second small cross is brought in and set to the other side.

G: It'd be great if anything would happen around here! Every day . . . out to the fields . . . plow, plow, plow . . . grab a quick lunch . . . back to work . . . crunch the grain . . . the same old grind. What kind of life is that?

C: It sure would be great if we could all go back to the good old days of shepherding like the Waltonbergs.

G: Are you kidding? I wouldn't go back to sheep for nothin'. Progress, man, progress. Oh sure, it gets a little dusty in town with all the traffic, but this is where the action is. Of course, all this activity has made my wife nag a little more (if that's possible).

C: I don't know, man. Seems like I just wake up, turn off my rooster, go to work, go home, blow out the lamp and go to bed. I wish there was something more. I'm beginning to wonder about all this religious stuff. I mean, if there is such a thing as God, why doesn't He just come down here and say, "Hi, folks. I'm God. How'd you like to see a few Romans made into pizza."

A third large cross is slowly brought in.

G: You ought to know by now, Cal, baby, religion is all a bunch of myths and stuff. Well, see you around.

C: OK, George, see you later.

G: (Sarcastically) Yeah. By the way, Cal, if you bump into some guy that says, "Hi, I'm God," let me know . . . I'd like to meet him.

THE FOOD STORE ROBBERY

This is an excellent "situation story" centered around the issue of stealing. There are many subtopics that can be discussed, such as the corporate structure, family stress, justice and law and order.

To use with your group, simply tell the story as it is presented below, and discuss the questions that are provided (or any other questions that may arise). You might find it useful to print up the story and distribute copies to each person. As you will discover, the circumstances of the story present some very difficult problems not unlike those that we have to deal with every day of our lives. The "answers" are not as clear as we would often like for them to be which is the beauty of an exercise such as this. It is through struggles with the hard questions that we grow and learn.

The story involves seven people:

1. The husband, Ed
2. The injured child
3. The teenage driver
4. The wife, Hilda
5. The plant manager
6. The banker
7. The food store owner

The Story:

The automobile factory where Ed has worked for the past ten years is experiencing hard times because of a recession and is forced to lay off a number of employees. Management has left the responsibility to each of the plant managers. Ed's plant manager has been protecting his job for a long time and has always been worried that Ed might get his job. He lays Ed off to remove this threat.

Ed cannot find a job anywhere. After eighteen months of unsuccessful job hunting, his unemployment runs out and Ed is forced to sell his insurance so his family can have food and make the house payments. When that money runs out, Ed and Hilda discuss the possibility of applying for welfare. Hilda will not hear of it. She considers it degrading and a sign of failure. In fact, Hilda considers Ed a failure and constantly nags him to do something about their situation. She threatens to leave him.

One evening, one of Ed's children is playing in the street. (The child had been warned many times to stay out of the street.) A stolen car driven by a nineteen-year-old runaway runs into Ed's child, seriously injuring him. The child requires hospitalization and the bills will be enormous. Of course, the runaway does not have any insurance or money.

In desperation, Ed goes to the bank to apply for a loan. Ed does have good credit, but the banker refuses the loan. (The banker has involved the bank's money in a number of questionable investments and has overextended the bank's loan limit.)

Ed explains the situation to Hilda. She explodes into a rage and hysterically threatens to leave and calls Ed a failure and a no-good who doesn't care about his child and his wife. She gives him an ultimatum to be gone when she returns and stomps out of the house. Distraught and confused, Ed robs the local food store. When his wife returns, he shows her the money and explains that a close friend loaned it to them. They use the money to purchase food and clothing for the children, but within a day Ed is arrested by the police. He explains, "All I wanted to do was feed my family."

After discussions with the city officials, the prosecutor decides to drop the case if Ed will pay back the money and seek counseling with the welfare department. But the store owner is a strong law and order advocate and refuses to drop the charges. He believes that Ed is a thief and ought to be punished. Ed is forced to go to trial where he pleads guilty and is sentenced by the judge.

Questions for Discussion:

1. Which person was most responsible for the robbery of the food store? Rank the characters from most responsible to least responsible. Give reasons for the order that you chose.
2. Was Ed wrong to rob the food store? Why or why not?
3. Hilda was certainly a nagging wife, but didn't she have something to nag about? Do you feel any compassion for Hilda?
4. Do you agree with Hilda's refusal to accept welfare?
5. What do you think Hilda did after Ed was arrested? What should she have done?
6. If you were the food store operator, would you press charges?
7. If you were the judge at the trial and Ed confessed to the crime, what sentence would you hand down?
8. Which person was the worst? Which was the best? Why?
9. What is your concept of "justice?"

FOTO-MATCH

Hang up twenty or so photos of people (all kinds . . . old, young, black, white, attractive, ugly, fat, slim, wealthy, poor, etc.). The first week the pictures are displayed, have the kids write descriptions of each person based on what they see in the picture. Collect them all during the following week, combine all the individual descriptions into a concise paragraph which accurately reflects the group consensus. Attach the descriptions to each picture for the next meeting. Have the students look at the photos with descriptions carefully (make sure they are numbered) and then answer the following questions:

1. Choose five people you would want to travel with for one year. Why?
2. Is there any one person you would not want anything to do with? Why?
3. Who, if any, would you be willing to marry?
4. Who, if any, would you worship with?
5. Which person do you think you could really like? Why?
6. If only five others and yourself were allowed to live and the others executed, which five would stay with you? Why?

You could have your group go through the questions again and decide how their parents would respond. And, of course, you can easily come up with other questions equally as good as these.

GETTING OLD ON CASSETTE

Have several of your youth group take tape recorders with them when they visit an elderly person (grandparent, member of the church, someone at the park, or a stranger). Be sure to get the person's permission before turning on the tape, and then ask questions on topics where age would be invaluable for insight into a specific problem. Suggested topics: friendship, marriage, love, death, grief, meaning, patience.

GOSPEL ACCORDING TO DEAR ABBY

Select from assorted "Dear Abby" and "Ann Landers" columns, letters which reflect problems relevant to your youth group. Then read one of the letters to your group (Note: If a large group, give one letter to each small group) *without the columnist's reply.* Then discuss how they think Jesus would have answered the letter. After sufficient discussion, read the columnist's reply and compare her answer with Jesus' hypothetical answer. Discuss the differences, if any.

Read as many letters as time allows, skipping the ones that don't generate any interest. Another twist to this would be to have each individual write his/her response to the Dear Abby letter and then compare each other's responses. Then using each person's letter as a resource, have the group compile a group letter combining the best elements of each individual letter.

GOSPEL NEWS

As a discussion starter, pass out parts of the daily newspaper to the kids as they arrive. Then ask them to find in the newspapers examples of where the "Gospel of Jesus Christ" is at work in the world, or where they think the Gospel is needed in a particular situation.

THE GREAT FISH CONTROVERSY

The following "parable" is excellent for stimulating discussion on evangelism and the ministry of the church:

> For months, the Fishers' Society had been wracked with dissension. They had built a new meeting hall which they called their Aquarium and had even called a world renowned Fisherman's Manual scholar to lecture them on the art of fishing. But still no fish were caught. Several times

each week they would gather in their ornate Aquarium Hall, recite portions of the Fisherman's Manual and then listen to their scholar exposite the intricacies and mysteries of the Manual. The meeting would usually end with the scholar dramatically casting his net into the large tank in the center of the hall and the members rushing excitedly to its edges to see if any fish would bite. None ever did, of course, since there were no fish in the tank. Which brings up the reason for the controversy. Why? The temperature of the tank was carefully regulated to be just right for ocean perch. Indeed, oceanography experts had been consulted to make the environment of the tank nearly indistinguishable from the ocean. But still no fish. Some blamed it on poor attendance to the Society's meetings. Others were convinced that specialization was the answer: perhaps several smaller tanks geared especially for different fish age groups. There was even division over which was more important: casting or providing optimum tank conditions. Eventually a solution was reached. A few members of the Society were commissioned to become professional fishermen and were sent to live a few blocks away on the edge of the sea and do nothing but catch fish. It was a lonely existence because most of the members of the Society were terrified of the ocean. So the professionals would send back pictures of themselves holding some of their catches and letters describing the joys and tribulations of real live fishing. And periodically they would return to Aquarium Hall to show slides. After such meetings, people of the Society would return to their homes thankful that their Hall had not been built in vain.

—*Ben Patterson*

HUMAN CONTINUUM

When discussing subjects that have many points of view, have the kids arrange themselves (prior to the discussion) on a "Human continuum" from one extreme viewpoint to the opposite extreme. For example, if you are discussing "drinking", have the kids line up with all those who are "for" drinking on one end, and those who are "against" it at the other. Undecideds or moderates would be somewhere in the middle.

FOR ── AGAINST

Kids may discuss the issue among themselves as they attempt to find the right spot in the line in relationship to each other. After they are settled, further discussion or debate can take place as kids attempt to defend their positions. Anyone may change positions at anytime.

INVENT

Divide your youth group into smaller groups of 8 to 10. Describe the situation below and give each group twenty minutes to finish their task. At the end of the allotted time, have the group all meet together and compare their responses.

Situation: You find yourself in a new civilization in which everything is the same as our world is now, but there is no Bible, no God, no religion, no church, no religious history. You have been selected by your government to create a God that will have the proper attributes that will cause people to worship. This God should represent everything that you think will be attractive and yet at the same time, explain things like natural disasters (flood, earthquake, etc.), sickness, suffering, and evil.

Questions to help you as you invent God: What is its name, if any? Where does it live? Is it visible? Will your God make any demands on people? How do you worship it? Any rewards or punishments? What does it look like? Is there more than one? Does it have any bad attributes? Just let your imaginations run wild and attempt to invent the "perfect" God that will attract the most people.

The discussion should then compare the invented God with the God of the Bible. The following questions could be included in the discussion:

1. Why is God so mysterious?
2. Why did God leave so many unanswered questions?
3. Why doesn't God make Himself visible?
4. What are the most difficult things about God to believe?
5. What things would you change about God if you could?

LABOR GAME

This game is based on the "Parable of the Labourers in the Vineyard" (Matthew 20:1-16). This sometimes perplexing parable can become real by allowing your youth to experience the frustration of the workers that complained about equal distribution of pay at the end of the day, even though all did not work as long or as hard. The owner (God) was just and kept his promise—paying exactly what He said He would. This would have satisfied the workers until greed crept in. The following simulation game will help kids to understand this parable more fully.

As the kids enter the room, have several tables prepared with a puzzle, "brain-teaser," or skill to do on each one. Some should be very easy, others impossible. Have points for each puzzle—depending on the difficulty, and each person is to keep track of his own score. After 20 or 30 minutes call a stop. Go to each young person, ask how many points he has, and then reach into a bag and give him a prize. The prize can be very small, just be sure every prize is exactly the same for everyone in the group.

As you slowly do this, it will soon be obvious to everyone in the group what is happening. No matter how high or low the score they tell you, they are all receiving equal payment. Allow free talk as you distribute the reward. Follow by discussion, prodding with questions such as "How do you honestly feel?"; "What is your attitude toward the "prize-giver?"; "How do you feel toward the other young people?" Ask the one that scored the highest and the one that scored the lowest how they feel. Follow by reading the scripture account of the parable and discuss greed, envy, lust, and competition, and how these things can foul up our relationships with God.

LAMED VOVNIK CONVENTION

There is a charming Jewish legend which states that the world exists due to the presence of only thirty-six righteous people. The Jewish name for these people is *lamed vov* (pronounced "lah-med vov"), which indicates thirty-six. These people may be of any station in life, poor or mighty, men or women, hermits or public figures. The only thing we know about them is that they are alive and that they do not know that they are *lamed vovniks*. If they claim to be, then they cannot be.

To conduct a "lamed vovnik convention," divide your group into as many small groups as you wish, and have each group nominate several individuals whom they think might qualify as a "lamed vovnik." They should be righteous, selfless, and the kind of persons on whom the welfare of the world might rest. Each group should take 10-15 minutes for this. Set a maximum number of people that each group may nominate.

When the groups have finished, have a "nominating convention." Each group announces its choices and explains why they nominated whom they did. A list can be kept on a blackboard, and a final vote can be taken to arrive at the entire group's guesses at who the thirty-six *lamed vovniks* are.

Many famous people will undoubtedly be nominated, but the beauty of the exercise is that many ordinary people, not well-known, will undoubtedly be favorites. At one "lamed vovnik convention" a man named David Rapaport was elected, when a persuasive young man nominated him with the words, "Most of you wouldn't know him, but when I need help or advice, he's always there to help me or steer me through times of trouble." Another notable nominee was an anonymous man on an immigrant ship who helped the father of one of the young people who said, "He gave dad some food and a little money, and did the same for many others on the boat. But no one remembers his name. . . ." Perhaps the best thing about the activity is the shift of emphasis from fame to humility. True models begin to emerge and kids begin to put some handles on what righteousness is all about.

LIFE LETTERS

Following a dicussion of "suicide," have kids write a "life letter" to a potential suicide victim, which expresses their reasons for their belief that life is worth living. After about twenty minutes of writing, have the kids share their letters with the rest of the group (if they want to). This gives some people a chance to share their faith and provide a unique learning experience as well.

LIVING CHRISTMAS GIFT

Here is a clever and meaningful Christmas gift suggestion that will become more valuable as the years go by. Have your young people interview their grandparents about their experiences in life. (Sort of an autobiography on tape.) Suggest that the young people duplicate the tape and give a copy to each of the relatives for Christmas.

LOOK AT THE BOOK

Here is a great discussion starter. The true/false statements below can be very effective in helping your young people determine their attitudes about the Bible and in helping you discover what your group thinks of the Bible.

Duplicate the following list of statements and have each member of your group take the test by writing "true" or "false" after each one. Then go back and discuss each question in detail.

1. The Bible is a record of man's search for God.
2. The Bible is like a scientific textbook when it describes the origin of the world.
3. The Bible is primarily a factual history of the Jewish people.
4. The Bible contains detailed answers to all of man's questions.
5. The Bible needs to be interpreted literally.
6. The main thrust of the Biblical witness is the description of ethical norms. (What is right and what is wrong.)
7. Every part of the Bible has the same level of importance as every other part.
8. One needs to read the Bible as a spectator rather than as a participant.

9. The Bible was written and compiled all at once.
10. All the writings in the Bible are a response to God's activity and concern for His people.
11. The Bible can prove the existence of God.
12. A person's job in studying the Bible is to learn to ask the right questions.
13. The Bible is a recital of history without interruption.
14. There is no other truth about God than what is disclosed in the Bible.
15. The Old Testament has no relevance for today.
16. The Bible is basically one story . . . that of God's search for communion with man.

LOVE GROUPS

This exercise is a five session project which is designed for more informal times with your youth group, although it could be used for Sunday School under certain conditions. The basic purpose is to let the youth be creative and imaginative about the subject of Christian love through many different activities. The teacher or youth leader acts as a traffic director and organizer and supplies very little direct lecture-type teaching.

The basic format of the five sessions has each youth working in an activity group for the first four sessions. Each of these activity groups is working on something directly related to the subject of Christian love. During the class period (while the activity groups are working), the leader stops all the groups for one of a variety of give-and-take sessions which include mini-lectures (3 minutes), discussion, a short film, or whatever, all dealing with the subject of love. The fifth session is devoted to presentation and action of each of the activity groups' finished products. (For example, the drama group would present their drama, and the "love banners" group would auction off their banners, etc.) Adults or other youth groups can be invited to the fifth session to see and hear the presentations.

Following are ten sample "love groups":

1. *The Signs of Love Slide Show:* This group will shoot pictures of "signs of love" all around them, have them developed, and create a slide show with narration or music.
2. *Drama:* This group will prepare a play on some facet of Christian love. It can be original, or it can be a well-known Bible story.
3. *The Multiple Listing Group:* This group will come up with lists centered around Christian love. For example, a list of "What love is," or "What it is not," or "Ways to demonstrate love," etc.
4. *The Crossword Puzzle Group:* This group will design one or more crossword puzzles based on the subject of Christian love.

5. *The Poetry Group:* This group will write original poetry about Christian love.
6. *The Cartoons Group:* This group will publish a booklet of Christian love cartoons. They can be original or from other publications.
7. *The Bible Scholar Group:* This group will research the concept of Christian love in the scriptures using commentaries, other books, etc., and write a report on the findings.
8. *The Love Banner Group:* This group must have some artistic and sewing ability, because they will produce banners on the subject of Christian love.
9. *The Songwriting Group:* This group will compose Christian love songs and perform them. They can be completely original or new words to familiar tunes.
10. *The Love Object Group:* This group will produce love-related art objects to auction off or give away, such as love necklaces, plaques, calligraphy, paintings, or whatever.

Each group should be supplied with the necessary items to complete their work and the kids should be encouraged to work at home on their project as well. A textbook (such as Francis Schaeffer's *The Mark of the Christian,* published by InterVarsity Press) can be used during the class sessions as a common study guide.

LUTTS AND MIPPS

Pretend that *lutts and mipps* represent a new way of measuring distance, and that *dars, wors, and mirs* represent a new way of measuring time. A man drives from Town "A" through Town "B" and Town "C" to Town "D." The task of your group is to determine how many *wors* the entire trip took. You have twenty minutes for this task. Do not choose a formal leader. You will be given bits of information that relates to the task of your group. You may share the information orally, but you must keep the written information in your hands throughout.

Divide into small groups of four or five and distribute the above instructions to each group. Then pass out one, two, or three cards to each person (they don't have to have the same number of cards, just shuffle and pass out all eight). The cards contain the information:

    Card 1: Town A is 16 lutts from Town C
    Card 2: Town B is 10 lutts, 6 mipps from Town D
    Card 3: Town C is halfway between Town B and Town D
    Card 4: The man is riding in a horse and buggy
    Card 5: The man's average speed is 1 lutt per dar
    Card 6: 10 wors equal 1 dar
    Card 7: 10 mipps equal 1 lutt
    Card 8: 10 mirs equal 1 wor

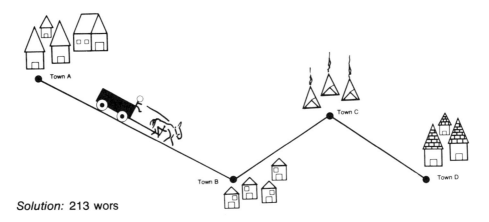

Solution: 213 wors

This, by the way, is a problem from a fourth grade math book. The problem solving experience shows us several things:

1. *Group dynamics:* Who was the leader? Why did you react the way you did? Did you feel a part of your group or like an outsider? Was there a sense of competition? Why or why not? How did you feel when the other group(s) finished before you? Etc. . . .

2. *Individual worth:* You have to sort out the information, which means you have to get all of it first. When working with youth, it is important to get all the information about them you can. This comes by being their friend and they begin to open up to you. You must use the right information and disregard the meaningless. (Have you ever noticed in board meetings that some guy always seems to think "But he's riding a horse and buggy" is the most important information?)

3. *Definition of terms:* We know the "lingo," but do we really know what it means? We toss around church words a lot, but do we take the time to ask ourselves and our youth, "What does that really mean?" Do we go through the motions without realizing what it means? And what about visitors to the group? Do we assume that they will know what "justification" or "communion" means or even who Jesus Christ is so that they leave confused because we didn't take the time to explain it to them? We need to discipline ourselves to talk the language that the people we try to communicate with can understand. And first, we need to clarify that meaning in our own life.

A MAD LATE DATE

The following is a short play which is useful for getting discussion going on the obvious areas of friction developed in the play as well as general family and parent-teen relationships.

Characters needed:
1. Father
2. Mother
3. Daughter (Christy)
4. Son (Donald)

The setting is the breakfast table. Everyone except Christy is seated. Father is reading the paper, Mother is pouring coffee, and Donald is toying with his cereal. Christy hasn't come in yet.

Mother: Quit playing with your food, Donald. You'll be late for school.

Father: I'll have some more coffee, dear.

Donald: Speaking of being late, what about Christy last night? Man, if I came in that late, I'd be flogged till daylight.

Father: You let us worry about your sister. Anyway, you have to be able to get a date first.

Donald: Funny, funny!

Mother: You know, I am worried about Christy. This is the third time this has happened and . . . (Christy enters and interrupts.)

Christy: . . . And every time there was a perfectly good excuse. Just like last night.

Donald: Some reasons! Out of gas, flat tires. . . What's it going to be this time?

Christy: It's none of your business, smart aleck.

Father: Well it is *my* business, Christy. You know how worried your mother and I become when you are late.

Mother: Yes, you could have at least called and let us know you had problems.

Donald: Kind of hard to find a phone booth out at Folsom Lake.

Christy: Knock it off, bird brain. I couldn't call. Coming home from the game we stopped at Eppie's and the service was just terrible . . .

Mother: Couldn't you have called from there?

Christy: No, Mom. We left in plenty of time—11:00. But we hit some traffic downtown because of the big fire. Just no way we knew that was going to happen.

Donald: Ha! That greaser you were with probably planned the whole thing.

Father: That's enough, Don. Christy, you know the rules around here. We've asked you to be in by 12:00 and this is the third time you've been late. I'm just going to have to put you on a one-week restriction.

Christy: But Dad you don't understand. We couldn't help it!

Father: I know you have a good reason, but rules are rules. And this isn't the first time.

Christy: So what if it is the fifteenth time? I couldn't help it and I don't think it's fair that I get restricted.

Donald: Fair? If it had been me, I would have been chained and muzzled to the bed post for a month!

61

Christy:	Yeah, you *should* be chained and muzzled with that mouth of yours.
Mother:	Regardless, Christy, we must have some rules and both of you have to obey them. I think your father is right. Anyway, I don't know if I like you dating that . . . that . . . oh, what is his name?
Donald:	You mean Greasy Gary?
Christy:	Shut up, Dummy! Now I know why I'm on restriction, you never have liked anybody I've dated. If it wasn't him, you'd find something else . . .
Father:	(Interrupts.) Now just a minute. The matter of liking who you're dating has nothing to do with it. I might say, however, you could be a little more choosey.
Christy:	Choosey! Who would you want me to date? One of those creeps at the church?
Mother:	Creeps? Where did you pick up that language?
Donald:	From Greasy Gary. I think that's his middle name.
Christy:	Okay, smart mouth . . .
Father:	Both of you calm down. If this is going to be your attitude, Christy, you can forget about going anywhere for the following week as well. Your mother and I could use a little help around here.
Christy:	WHAT, YOU CAN'T BE SERIOUS! What about Donald? All he does is sit around and flap his mouth making corny jokes.
Mother:	Now, Christy, that's enough. There's no need to bring your brother into this. I think it is time we be just a little more considerate of each other.
Christy:	Why don't you start with me? I come in a lousy 45 minutes late and you act like it was three hours. Then you start harping on who I date. All you're concerned about is your silly rules and regulations.
Father:	You don't need to raise your voice to your mother. And rules and regulations are something to be concerned about. But more important is your behavior to those rules. Either you shape up or else.
Donald:	Or shape out . . . that shouldn't be hard for you.
Christy:	(in tears) I've had enough! I'm leaving! Nobody understands me. You just don't care.
Mother:	We do care Christy. You are the one who doesn't understand. Why, when I was your age . . .
Christy:	Now comes the second lecture! Well, times are different and you are *not my age!*
Father:	I think I've heard enough. Both of you get off to school, and Christy . . . I want you home at 4:00 sharp.

THE MORAL OF THE STORY . . .

Read a story (proverb, fable, Biblical, or make-believe) and leave out the "moral" at the end, if there is one. Challenge each person to write down what he thinks the moral of the story could be. They can then share them and discuss. It's amazing how many different things you can learn from one simple story.

PARABLE OF THE SHAPES

The following play is excellent for use in conjunction with a discussion or meeting with a "love" theme. It is based on the idea that there are basically three kinds of love: "if" love, "because" love, and "in-spite-of" love (which is the best kind, of course).

The characters each carry a large cardboard shape as their costume. Their identities thus become their shapes. The "Blob" should carry a crumpled-up newspaper or some other nondescript shape, and the "In-spite-of" Man carries no shape at all.

The Script:

Narrator:
There once was a land of If and Because
That sat on the earth as every land does.
And every person who lived in the land
Would search for a person he could understand
Now let us together observe what takes place
When If and Because people meet face-to-face . . .

1st Circle:
As I walk along this fine sunny day,
A stranger I see coming my way.
Is he a friend or is he a foe?
Not till I look at his shape will I know.
A circle I be and a circle I stay.
A circle is needed for friendship today.
(Enter the Blob.)
Hello my friend, Circle's my name
And finding a friend is my kind of game.
Have you a circle to exchange with me here?
Or are you an alien shape, I fear?

Blob:
A friendly fellow you seem to be
And circles I need for good friends to be.
What my own shape is, I really don't know
But I hope it's a circle so friendship will grow.
I'm so glad I found you, I'm so glad to see
That such a relationship can possibly be.

1st Circle:
Now wait a minute, oh stranger here.
You hasten your happiness too fast I fear.
I told you before our two shapes must match
In order for any new friendship to hatch.
If you were a circle with roundest of frame,
We'd be friends forever because we're the same.
But I see no circle, I see nothing round.
I think that it's only a Blob that I've found.

63

Now think of my image, what others might say,
I can't take the risk. Away! Away!

Blob:
I'm so broken hearted, I'm in such despair.
I am not a circle. It doesn't seem fair.
(Enter 2nd Circle.)

2nd Circle:
A call for a circle, is that what I hear?
I too am a circle, such joy and such cheer!
For now, brother Circle, your long vigil ends.
We've found one another. Forever we're friends!
(Two circles embrace and walk off.)

1st Star:
I am a star, a beautiful star.
Better than all other shapes, by far.
And if you are the finest, I think you will see
That shape you are holding, a star it will be.
If I'd find a star, we'd frolic in fun
And dance and play and never be done.
If you are a star, my friendship you've won.

But as I look closer, I see you're not one.
You're only a Blob! We'll never go far,
Unless you can prove that you're also a star!

Blob: My shape's not important. Myself is what counts.
Just give me some friendship in any amount.

1st Star: I've no time for Blobs, so go on your way,
For I think a star is coming this way . . .
(Enter 2nd star.)

2nd Star: A star I am, and a star I'll stay.
Oh praise be to stars, it's our lucky day!

1st Star: O star, O star, what double delight!
These shapes that we're holding, they match us just right.

2nd Star: At last we're together, so happy and proud.
Together we'll surely stand out in a crowd.
So Blob, adios! Farewell and goodbye!
You just don't fit in, and don't ask us why.

Blob: Alas, I am broken. What worse could I do?
Than being rejected by each of these two.
(Enter 1st square.)

1st Square: Through this crowd I now will stare
To see if perhaps there be somewhere a square.
Pardon me there, but some time could you lend?
If you are a square, I'll be your true friend.

Blob:	Oh surely, dear brother, our shape's not the same, But I'm a sweet person, and what's in a name?
1st Square:	Your shape's not a square and you talk to me so? I can't believe all the nerve that you show. If it's friendship you want, then friendship go get. But not from a shape with which you don't fit! *(Enter 2nd square.)*
2nd Square:	A call for a square? I'll soon be right there? A square I am and a square I'll be. I'll join you in friendship, oh square, just ask me. Because our fine corners do each number four, We'll stay close together forever and more! *(They both exit.)*
Blob:	I'm torn and I'm frazzled, what worse could there be, Than being rejected by each of these three. *(Enter 1st Triangle.)*
1st Triangle:	I'm wandering to and I'm wandering fro, In search of a three-sided shape just like so. *(points)* For if I could find one, I know we would blend, For only a triangle can be a true friend.
Blob:	Hello there, dear fellow, I've heard all you've said, I can't help but thinking, to you I've been led. For you need friendship and I need the same. So on with the friendship and off with the game.
1st Triangle:	Now who is this talking? What shape do you hold? You seem sort of strange, just what is your mold? You sure are not pretty, you shapeless disgrace. Why, you're just a Blob, it's all over your face! I've no time for you, you pitiful one. This senseless discussion is over and done! *(Enter 2nd Triangle.)*
2nd Triangle:	A call for triangles? Well I'll fill the need. We're made for each other, it must be agreed! *(They exit together.)*
Blob:	No one understands poor shapeless me, Cause I'm just a Blob as you can well see.

66

If I were a circle or maybe a square,
Then I could be having some fun over there.
Why can't all you shapes just notice and see,
That I'm just as miserable as I can be.
With no one to laugh and be good friends with,
I'm beginning to feel just a little bit miffed.

Narrator: Now just at this moment comes into this place
A man who is different in style and in grace.
He's quiet and thoughtful and listens quite well,
Observing the stories that our characters tell.
Now with me return to our tale if you can,
And witness the ways of "In-Spite-Of" Man.
(Enter In-Spite-Of Man.)

In-Spite-Of Man: Hello, will you be my friend?

Blob: Oh, no, can't you see . . .
I'm not a circle or square, so please leave me be.

In-Spite-Of Man: Friend, once again to you I will say,
Will you not be my friend on this fine, day?

Blob: Your humor's not funny, I'm wise to your jokes.
You're here to make fun like the rest of these folks.

In-Spite-Of Man: Now what is the problem, my poor little man?
You seem so distressed, I just can't understand.

Blob:	I've run the whole gamit, I've pleaded and cried To have them accept me and love me inside. But each time I seek them they look at my shape, And quickly reject me, it's like hearing a tape. "You're not the right person, you've got the wrong shape, The people will gossip, the people will gape." If this shall continue from day unto day, Alone I'll remain and depressed will I stay.
In-Spite-Of Man:	I think a great lesson's been brought to your sight. These shapes find it hard to accept you "in spite". They're all so possessive and selfish inside, They wallow in vanity, ego, and pride. But there is an answer I've found to be true, And I've come to offer this answer to you.
Blob:	I don't understand all you're trying to say, But you're the first person I've met here today Who seems to accept me in spite of my form You break all the rules of the shape-seekers norm.
In-Spite-Of Man:	Your wisdom is growing, I think you now see Love puts no conditions on you or on me.
Narrator:	Our moral is simple, I'll share it with you. It's all in the Bible and known to be true. The world offers values which dazzle our eyes, It mixes the truth with ridiculous lies. And we here are seeking the true meaning of This life that we're living, this word we call "love". The If and Because folks are caught in a bind, For they only accept their very own kind. They love folks "because" and they love people "if", But few have discovered the "In-Spite-Of" Gift!

PAUL'S DILEMMA

The following is a contrived situation involving a teenage boy named Paul. He faces a problem for which he receives "advice" from friends and relatives holding various points of view. This situation can be either read to the group by the leader or acted out in a sort of role play. After presenting the situation to the group including all the advice which Paul receives, discuss the questions provided with the entire group.

The Situation:

Paul is a junior in high school. He is relatively well accepted by his friends. He makes average grades and is a member of several school organizations: choir, the basketball team and student council. He has been friends with one group of five guys through most of his junior high and high school years. His parents are respectable members of the community. His father is a lawyer and his mother the secretary of a popular civic organization. The whole family is active in a local church where his father and mother hold leadership positions.

Paul's problem is this: he has been close with this group of five guys for a long time and their values have always been quite similar. But lately, the guys have been experimenting with drugs and alcohol. Although Paul has participated until now, he is beginning to feel more and more uncomfortable. He has discussed the problem with his buddies and they do not feel uncomfortable. If Paul decides to stop going along with the group, it may cost him his relationship with the guys. He approaches a number of acquaintances seeking advice:

Youth Group Sponsor: He is concerned that Paul may get sucked into the habits of his buddies. His advice is to break the relationship pointing out that Jesus never allowed relationships to get in the way of his convictions. He refers to others (such as Martin Luther) who did what they knew was right regardless of the circumstances.

Paul's Uncle: His favorite uncle who is also a lawyer, listens nervously as Paul confides that he really doesn't see what is so wrong with all of these things. It's just that he doesn't feel right. Paul's uncle immediately attempts to point out through statistics the dangers of marijuana and alcohol. He attempts to rationally investigate all of the "phony" justifications for using grass and alcohol and makes a case for abstinence, the only really logical and safe conclusion.

Sunday School Teacher: He points out that you are either "with" Christ or "against" him. You either are committed or not committed. What is at stake is behaving like a Christian should and renouncing every "appearance of evil" or capitulating and being "worldly" and "sold out" to sin.

Youth Director: He relates to Paul a true story of a close friend who was bothered by the direction his friends were going, but didn't have enough courage to stand for his conviction. The result was that he became heavily involved in drugs, disgraced his family and friends and eventually committed suicide. He suggests that Paul has great potential to influence hundreds of young people and he could blow his chances of potential greatness. In fact, the youth director confides, he was just going to ask Paul to take a leadership position in the group.

A Neighbor (who is also a policeman): He confronts Paul with the fact that he saw a report on some of Paul's friends who were on the brink of getting into trouble with drugs, etc. The neighbor is concerned that Paul understand the legal implications of his friends' behavior and counsels him to stay away lest he and his friends get busted. He then goes on to explain that he personally does not see what's wrong with a kid experimenting with marijuana, but that we must all obey the laws otherwise there would be total chaos. Laws are there for our protection and we must follow them.

The Pastor: He points out that the church has always spoken out against "non-Christian behavior" and that ever since the church was founded such things were not acceptable for church members. The purity of the church, whether it's local body of believers or "the church universal," has always been a focal point for "our doctrine."

His Girlfriend: She points out that she does not care what anyone else says, he must do what's right. If he made the wrong choice, he would never be able to live with himself. She reminds him that if his parents knew he was experimenting with marijuana and alcohol, "his mother would be crushed" and "his father would be humiliated." "Besides," she says, "What about me and our relationship? You know what I think of your group of friends and what they are doing, and if I meant very much to you, you would think carefully about what you're doing."

Paul's Older Brother: He thinks Paul is too narrow and making an issue out of nothing. He feels Paul is experiencing false guilt produced by the unenlightened view of their parents. He points out that he regularly smokes pot and drinks and still maintains a high grade point average and also holds down a good job. He counsels Paul not to get involved in heavy drugs or excessive drinking, but warns him not to sacrifice his good friendships for a "non-issue."

Questions for Discussion:

1. Evaluate each of the arguments given to Paul. What are the strengths, if any, and what are the weaknesses, if any?
2. Which person do you most agree with? Why? Least agree with? Why?
3. What answer would have have given Paul? What would you do in Paul's situation?
4. Is there a "right answer" to Paul's Dilemma?
5. What were Paul's alternatives?
6. If Paul had weighed all the alternatives and made what you considered to be a wrong choice, what would you say to Paul if you were:

a. a close friend
b. a girlfriend
c. a parent
d. a brother/sister

e. a youth director
f. a minister
g. a school counselor

POOR MAN'S HOLY LAND TOUR

You can have a "Poor Man's Holy Land Tour" by taking kids and/or adults on a tour of places within walking or riding distance inside your city. This includes taking them to the tallest building and having a Bible study there about Satan's temptation for Jesus to jump from the high mountain. It also includes a trip to an over-grown old cemetery where we would study about the man from Gadara. The options are end-less: a city jail, a motel bedroom (David's sin), Jewish Synagogue, mountainside (for Sermon on the Mount), garden (for Garden of Gethsemane), upstairs room in some home (for the last supper), old boiler room (for the story of the Jewish children in the fiery furnace), on the roadside (for the story of the good Samaritan or Paul's conver-sion experience), a lakefront or a wilderness area (depending on where you live). The possibilities are endless and the impression made in the study usually beats most other audio visual techniques combined.

PRIORITY AUCTION

Following is a delightful way of enabling a youth group to set priorities in their plans for future programs, without having to first overcome the usual resistence to the work that this task entails. This procedure could also be used for any process of "rank ordering" or "priority setting."

1. Create some paper "money" for the group to use, or else borrow some from a board game (or print various numerical values on 3 X 5 cards with a check writing machine to make the "money" you want).
2. Distribute the "money" in equal proportions to the group members.
3. Distribute a list of the tasks, programs, or whatever is to be ranked according to priorities to the group members.
4. Explain that the list is like a catalogue issued before an art auction, and that the members are going to bid on each item listed. The members can bid individually or pool their "money" and bid as small groups, but they can spend during the auction only as much money as they have been given. This will mean that each member must rank in his own mind which items are most valuable to him, and bid accordingly.
5. Make sure that each member understands each item listed, and then proceed with the auction, item by item. Make sure to collect the money from the top bidder as each item is sold, and list the selling price. This list, giving relative amounts in

dollar value, can then be a means of ranking the items according to the group's sense of priorities.

PROBLEM HOT LINE

Have the group sit in a circle with two chairs back to back in the center of the circle. Choose two people; one to be the Hotline worker, the other a caller with a problem. The worker leaves the room while the group leader assigns a problem to the caller. When the worker returns, the caller pretends to call the worker and explain his problem. It is important that the worker and caller remain back to back. The group leader is responsible for cutting the mock call off at the proper time and leading a discussion among the rest of the group as to how the problem might be solved. Some examples of problems:

1. I am not very attractive. People avoid me and I can tell that most of the people I know make fun of me behind my back. Frankly, I'm ugly. I know it and so does everyone else. So what can I do?

2. My parents make me go to church. I like the youth program, but the worship service is a drag. Our minister is irrelevant and boring and the services don't relate to me at all.

3. My mother is dying of cancer. Every day I am faced with cancer's ugly and depressing toll on my mom. I am forced to accept more and more of her responsibilities at home. But I like to go out with my friends too. I feel guilty when I go somewhere and have a good time, but if I stay home I get angry and frustrated. What's the answer?

4. I have always been told that kids who smoke grass and drink really don't enjoy it. So I have refrained from doing those things partly because I believed that and partly because I didn't think it was a Christian thing to do. At least until a few weeks ago. I have tried pot and drinking and it was great. I never had so much fun in my life. How can something so good be bad? Were the people who told me how bad these things were lying?

RECYCLED HYMNS

Have your group go through your church hymnal and choose their favorite hymns. Then spend a meeting or two rewriting the words. Mimeograph the best ones and sing in your youth meetings or with the adults in the main service. These recycled hymns might become so well liked that they become a regular part of your worship.

RUN FOR YOUR LIFE

Although this strategy deals with the subject of death, it is really about life and how we live it. The purpose of this exercise is to help young people to evaluate their priorities in light of what is really important. It allows the group to contrast what they are doing now with what they would do if they only had one month to live. Give each person in the group a list similar to the one below.

If I only had one month to live, I would:
1. Perform some high risk feat that I have always wanted to do, figuring that if I don't make it, it won't really matter.
2. Stage an incredible robbery for a large amount of money which I would immediately give to the needy and starving of the world.
3. Not tell anyone.
4. Use my dilemma to present the gospel to as many people as I could.
5. Spend all my time in prayer and Bible reading.
6. Make my own funeral arrangements.
7. Offer myself to science to be used for experiments that might have fatal results.
8. Have as much fun as possible (sex, parties, booze, whatever turns me on).
9. Travel around the world and see as much as possible.
10. Buy lots of stuff on credit that I've always wanted: expensive cars, fancy clothes, exotic food, etc. ("Sorry, the deceased left no forwarding address.")
11. Spend my last month with my family or close personal friends.
12. Not do anything much different. Just go on as always.
13. Isolate myself from everyone, find a remote place and meditate.
14. Write a book about my life (or last month).
15. Sell all my possessions and give the money to my family, friends, or others who need it.
16. _____ (fill in your own).

Have the group rank these alternatives (plus any they wish to add) from first to last choice. The first item on their list would be the one they would probably do, and the last would be the one they would probably not do. Have everyone share their choices, explain why they chose that way, and then discuss the results with the entire group. Another way to evaluate the alternatives is to put each one on a continuum. On one end of the continuum would be "Yes, definitely" and on the other end, "Absolutely not." After each alternative is placed on the continuum, compare and discuss with the rest of the group.

Yes, definitely   Absolutely not

SCREWTAPE LETTERS

This exercise is a good way to make the kids think about a topic by coming in through the back door. Divide them into groups of about five kids each and assign a recorder who is given pen and paper. Explain to the kids what a "Screwtape Letter" is and if you own the book (*Screwtape Letters* by C. S. Lewis), read a few excerpts so that they get the idea. Next, have them write a Screwtape Letter on "How To Destroy a Christian's Prayer Life" or a similar topic. In the process, they must consider what makes a good prayer life before they can write down how to destroy it. If you want, you can have them first of all list five or ten things necessary for a good prayer life and then work on those. Most kids love to show how devious they can be anyway, and in the process of being devious and creative, they have to consider what constitutes an effective prayer life. Have each group read theirs and then discuss.

THE SERMON OF THE MOUSE

The following article can be read aloud to the group or it can be printed and passed out to each person. It raises some important issues concerning the church and should be discussed using the questions that follow or others that you may want to add.

The Sermon of the Mouse:

The day had finally arrived. Everyone in the congregation was waiting expectantly. The negotiations had taken months, but finally everything had been worked out. It wasn't every congregation in the country that could have an opportunity like this. It was a rare visit from a very well known celebrity.

The pastor and his guest mounted the platform. The first hymn was sung. Then the pastor rose, "I'm sure everyone is aware who our guest speaker is this morning," he said.

Aware? How could anyone help being aware? There were posters all over town. There was a big yellow and black banner stretched across the entry to the parking lot. Seating in the sanctuary had been done on a reservation basis with preferential treatment given to members of the congregation in good standing. An overflow crowd was watching the service on closed circuit television. Everybody knew about it.

"It isn't often," said the pastor, "that we have an opportunity to meet someone who has become a legend in his own time. Starting back in the bleak years of the depression with a shoe string budget and a very simple plan, our guest, with hard work and contagious enthusiasm, built an empire for himself that rivals that of Howard Hughes. His name is a household word, he is admired by young and old alike, and he has even survived his mentor. He reigns over a multi-million dollar business venture that was so successful in Southern California that he established an even more spectacular venture in Florida. By now, I'm sure you know who I am talking about. We are so honored to have Mickey Mouse with us today to share with us the secrets of Disneyland's success with the hope that our church will be stimulated and helped by his story."

A hush came over the congregation as this famous mouse rose to his feet, cleared his throat, and began his sermon.

"Thank you for inviting me to come to your church. I must admit at first I was surprised that a church would ask me to give a sermon. Oh, I have been invited to Sunday School contests where they give each new person a Mickey Mouse Hat and expect me to shake hands with everyone and act funny, but a sermon is something new.

"But after I thought about it, I realized that maybe Disneyland and the church did have a lot in common and as I began to organize my thoughts, I saw how ingenious it was to invite me to share. I really believe that if your church were to apply our principles you could become as successful as Disneyland.

"First, make sure your enterprise seems exciting, even dangerous, but be quick to let your people know that there really is no danger involved. *Give the illusion of great risk,* but make sure everything is perfectly safe.

"Second, admit that you are in the entertainment business. People won't care what you say as long as they're entertained. Keep your people happy. Don't tell them anything negative. And don't make demands on them. Just keep them diverted from the ugly reality of today's world and they will keep coming back for more.

"Third, make everything look religious. Make the religious experience so elaborate, so intricate, so complex that only the professionals can pull it off and all the laymen can do is stand around with their mouths open and watch. People would rather watch an imitation mechanical bird sing than they would a real bird anyway. They would rather watch worship than do it.

"Fourth and finally, pretend that there are no problems. At Disneyland we dress our security guards up as smiling rabbits or friendly bears because we don't want anyone's experience at Disneyland to be ruined by the sight of law enforcement personnel. Disguise your problems and failures behind a warm smile and a firm handshake. Leave them at home and let the church be a happy place where there aren't any ugly problems. Just friendly pastors and smiling deacons.

"People today want good clean entertainment. They want an environment that is safe for children and they want a place that is safe for their family and friends. I am so glad to see that the church is moving in this direction. Thank you and God bless you."

Questions for discussion:
1. What parallels, if any, do you see between Disneyland and the organized church?
2. Analyze each of the mouse's points. Below are some questions that may help:

   "Give the illusion of great risk, but make everything safe."
   a. Are there any risks involved in being a Christian today?
   b. Does modern Christianity really cost the Christian anything?
   c. Can you think of any examples of the church creating an "illusion" or risk?
   d. How, if at all, does a church make people "safe"?

   "Entertain the people."
   a. How do churches "entertain" their people?
   b. Should Christianity and the church be entertaining?
   c. React to this statement: "People today must be entertained. After all, they have become sophistocated by watching the professional entertainment on television and at the movies. The church is competing for a person's time and attention and must give them something to make them want to come. After they get there, then they can be given spiritual content.

   "Make everything look religious."
   a. Define "religious."

76

b. What do you think Mickey Mouse meant by "religious"?

"Pretend there are no problems."

a. Do you think the church should admit to having problems? The pastor? The people?
b. How can a church pretend it doesn't have any problems?
c. If Christianity is true, then don't problems raise doubts in the minds of searching unbelievers?

SOLOMON'S COLLAGE

Conduct a study of Ecclesiastes 2 which describes Solomon's vain experimentation with pleasure (sex, entertainment, alcohol), possessions (homes, lands, wealth), and even the accumulation of wisdom and knowledge. This can be compared with how modern advertising still tries to convince the public that these same things are the "answer" to life and the pursuit of happiness. Distribute magazines, scissors, marking pens, and glue to the group and have them compose collages using advertisements and quotes from the scripture text to communicate what they learned. This can result in a very impressive and thought-provoking display for the church lobby or youth meeting room.

SPIRITUAL GIFT LIST

Make a list of all the "gifts of the spirit" found in Ephesians 4, 1 Corinthians 12, and Romans 12. Then have everyone in the group "rank order" the gifts from most important to least important and explain why they made their choices. Then discuss in light of Paul's advice in 1 Cor. 12:31 to "earnestly desire the greater gifts."

SUICIDE ROLE PLAY

The following role play is excellent as a way to make young people aware of the feelings of people contemplating suicide, and to help them develop counseling skills as well.

Select a group of kids from your youth group and divide them in half. One half of the group is to individually research and develop a character who is suicidal. They should do this thoroughly, so that they can answer any question put to them. Each person in this "suicidal" group should have a different motivation for wanting to take his own life, if possible.

The second half of the group is to research various counseling techniques that could be used in dealing with a person considering suicide. When the two groups come together at the meeting, set up some toy telephones, one for each group, and have the two groups send a person in, one at a time. The suicidal person calls the "Help Line," where a counselor is ready to answer. The two carry on a dialogue until either the problem is resolved, or a point is reached where the conversation cannot go any further (no progress is being made). Then have the group discuss and evaluate techniques used in counseling, whether or not such a conversation could have ever taken place, and make suggestions as to approaches they might have taken.

TOUR OF YOUR LIFE

This day-long field trip is great with junior highs and gives them an opportunity to view life somewhat more completely and realistically. Begin by visiting the maternity ward of a local hospital (prearranged, of course) where the kids can see newborns and their parents. Perhaps a doctor can tell about the birth process and give a brief tour of the area. Next, take the kids to a local college or university campus, and show them around. The next stop should be a factory or shop where people are at work. At this point, the need for work and the types of work available can be discussed. Then proceed to a convalescent home or some other place where senior citizens live and visit with the older folks. Allow the kids to share with them in some way and allow the seniors to also share with the kids in some way. The last stop on the tour should be a mortuary or funeral home. The funeral director may show the kids around, explain what happens to the body when it is brought in; the types of caskets available, and so on. Close the experience with a meeting or discussion in the funeral chapel (if there is one) or elsewhere if you wish. Other places can be added to this tour depending on how much time you have or the types of places available to you. Allow kids to think about their own lives, the kind of life that they want, and how they are going to achieve their goals.

THE WINDOW

Read or tell the following story to the group.

The Window

There were once two men, Mr. Wilson and Mr. Thompson, both seriously ill in the same room of a great hospital. Quite a small room, just large enough for the pair of them. Two beds, two bedside lockers, a door opening on the hall, and one window looking out on the world.

Mr. Wilson, as part of his treatment, was allowed to sit up in bed for an hour in the afternoon (something to do with draining the fluid from his lungs). His bed was next to the window. But Mr. Thompson had to spend all of his time flat on his back. Both of them had to be kept quiet and still, which was the reason they were in the small room by themselves. They were grateful for the peace and privacy, though. None of the bustle and clatter and prying eyes of the general ward for them. Of course, one of the disadvantages of their condition was that they weren't allowed to do much: no reading, no radio, certainly no television. They just had to keep quiet and still, just the two of them.

Well, they used to talk for hours and hours. About their wives, their children, their homes, their jobs, their hobbies, their childhood, what they did during the war, where they'd been on vacations, all that sort of thing. Every afternoon, when Mr. Wilson, the man by the window, was propped up for his hour, he would pass the time by describing what he could see outside. And Mr. Thompson began to live for those hours.

The window apparently overlooked a park with a lake where there were ducks and swans, children throwing them bread and sailing model boats, and young lovers walking hand in hand beneath the trees. And there were flowers and stretches of grass, games of softball, people taking their ease in the sunshine, and right at the back, behind the fringe of trees, there was a fine view of the city skyline. Mr. Thompson would listen to all of this, enjoying every minute. How a child nearly fell into the lake, how beautiful the girls were in their summer dresses, then an exciting ball game, or a boy playing with his puppy. It got to the point that he could almost see what was happening outside.

Then one fine afternoon when there was some sort of a parade, the thought struck him: Why should Wilson, next to the window, have all the pleasure of seeing what was going on? Why shouldn't *he* get the chance? He felt ashamed and tried not to think like that, but the more he tried, the worse he wanted a change. He would do anything! In a few days, he had turned sour. *He* should be by the window. He brooded. He couldn't sleep and grew even more seriously ill which the doctors just couldn't understand.

One night as he stared at the ceiling, Mr. Wilson suddenly woke up, coughing and choking, the fluid congesting in his lungs, his hands groping for the call button that would bring the night nurse running. But Mr. Thompson watched without moving. The coughing racked the darkness. On and on. He choked and then stopped. The sound of breathing stopped. Mr. Thompson continued to stare at the ceiling.

In the morning, the day nurse came in with water for their baths and found Mr. Wilson dead. They took his body away quietly with no fuss.

As soon as it seemed decent, Mr. Thompson asked if he could be moved to the bed next to the window. So they moved him, tucked him in, made him quite comfortable, and left him alone to be quiet and still. The minute they'd gone, he propped himself up on one elbow, painfully and laboriously, and strained as he looked out the window.

It faced a blank wall.

Discussion:

This beautiful story is not only an excellent illustration for a talk (on a variety of subjects) with its surprise twist at the end, but lends itself well for good discussion possibilities. The following questions raise some of the issues, but are only suggestions and do not have to be followed in any order, nor do all the questions have to be covered. Feel free to develop your own.

1. What was your initial reaction to the story? Were you shocked? Surprised? Angry?
2. From the story, describe Mr. Wilson. What kind of man does he appear to be? Do you like or dislike him? Why?
3. Describe Mr. Thompson. What kind of person is he? Do you like or dislike him?
4. Why did Mr. Wilson do what he did? What do you think his motives were?
5. Would you describe Mr. Wilson's "descriptions" of what was outside the window as: (a) lying? (b) creative imagination? (c) unselfish concern for Mr. Thompson? (d) cruel and envy producing? (e) _____.
6. Did Mr. Wilson do anything wrong?
7. Why did Mr. Thompson's mood change from enjoyment and appreciation to resentment? Was his resentment justified?
8. Did Mr. Thompson *murder* Mr. Wilson?
9. Who was guilty of the more serious wrong? Mr. Wilson or Mr. Thompson?
10. Who was most responsible for Mr. Wilson's death? Why?
11. Would both men have been better off without Mr. Wilson's descriptions of the view outside the window?
12. If you had been Mr. Thompson, how would you have felt when you finally looked out the window and saw nothing but a blank wall? (a) disappointed? (b) angry? (c) guilty? (d) grieved? (e) grateful? (f) puzzled? (g) shocked?
13. Is it a sin to fantasize?
14. Is it a sin to hide the truth or to exaggerate when it doesn't hurt anyone?
15. Where does one draw the line in the areas of fantasy and imagination?

WORSHIP DIARY

This is an idea designed to enrich your group's worship experience and at the same time receive some constructive feedback on this most important area in the church's life. Have each member in your group begin a worship diary in which he writes his response to the worship service. Kids should be writing their responses to questions like, How did I feel? Was I bored? Happy? Moved? What was the response of the people around me? What was most helpful? Least helpful? Did I learn anything? If so, what? Did I feel restricted or inhibited? Did the sermon help me at all? Have the group keep the diary for about four weeks and then have a meeting where everyone compares notes. The discussion following could be quite enlightening.

YOUTH GROUP DEVOTIONAL

Instead of using daily devotional guides published by your denomination, have your youth group write their own. This gives the young people a chance to express their ideas about the Christian faith. Most importantly, the kids will want to read the devotionals because they know the authors and they can relate to their own peers better. Of course, you could follow any format you want.

Here are two samples:

TUESDAY

Ephesians 6:2

"Honor thy father and mother."

Even though parent-child relationships are not always the best, each one of us owe a lot to our mothers and fathers. From the time we were born, our parents have loved and cared for us. My parents have done a lot for me and they are both very special. Often though, I take them for granted and I don't take time to tell them I love them.

I could do many small things to show them I care. What keeps me from showing them that I need and cherish them? I really don't know. I do know that I love them, need them, owe a lot to them, and should not take them for granted. To honor my parents would mean simply to love and respect them. Today and everyday, I want to show them just how special they are to me and how much I care.

Anita Cassis

THOUGHT: For a few minutes think about all your parents have done for you, given you, and cared for you. Today show them how special they are to you. Show them love, and thank God if they are still alive, that you have this day to live with them.

WEDNESDAY

Matthew 7:1-2

"Don't criticize, and you won't be criticized.
For others will treat you as you treat them."

This is another one of those verses that I feel everyone should follow. Before I read this verse, I never realized that one reason people use to criticize me so much was because I criticized them! And I did. I found myself telling people they had bad tempers, etc., but it never even crossed my mind to think I had a bad temper! So next time you go to criticize someone, stop and think, are you really perfect enough to criticize another person?

Kim Francis

THOUGHT: We really need one another as we walk in our everyday life. We can add so much to one another as we share our love and importance with each other. Today, tell someone in person, and on the phone, how much you need him, and how thankful you are that he is part of your world.

4 | Special Events

ACTION SCAVANGER HUNT

Here is another creative variation of a scavenger hunt. Each person (or team) receives a list similar to the one below and goes door-to-door as in a normal scavenger hunt. At each house the person at the door is asked to perform one of the actions on the list. If he complies, that item can be crossed off. The team with the most crossed off at the end of the time limit, or the first team to complete the entire list, is the winner. Only one item may be done at each house.

1. Sing two verses of "Old MacDonald."
2. Do 10 jumping jacks.
3. Recite John 3:16.
4. Name 5 movies currently playing at local theatres.
5. Yodel something.
6. Run around your house.
7. Start your car's engine and honk the horn.
8. Take our picture.
9. Whistle "Yankee Doodle" all the way through.
10. Say the Pledge of Allegiance.
11. Give us a guided tour of your back yard.
12. Autograph the bottom of our feet.
13. Say "bad blood" ten times very fast.
14. Burp.
15. Do a somersault.

BICYCLE PEDDLEMONIUM DAY

This is a fun event that can involve the entire youth department in an exciting day full of bike activities. Divide the action into three separate parts: (1) A Bicycle Olympics (2) A Bike Road Rally and (3) A Bike Tour. Begin around noon on a Saturday (or a Holiday) and run all the activities during the afternoon.

The Bicycle Olympics:

Divide the group into four competing groups if you have junior high through college age involved: (a) Junior high boys (b) Junior high girls (c) Senior high and college boys (d) Senior high and college girls. Points and prizes can be awarded the winners in each division. Some sample events:

1. *100 Yard Dash:* A race for time. Use a stopwatch.
2. *20 Lap Endurance Race:* Should be about five miles on a regular quarter-mile track. Award points to first through fifth places.
3. *Backward Race:* Should be optional. Kids ride with their backs to the front tire.
4. *Figure Eight Race:* Set up a figure eight track and contestants ride it, one at a time, for best clocked time.
5. *Obstacle Race:* Set up a track with obstacles, mud, trees, or whatever, to make riding difficult.
6. *Bike Jousting:* Bike riders ride toward each other in parallel lanes. Each rider gets a water balloon. The object is to ride by your opponent and hit him with the balloon, without getting hit yourself. Winners advance.

Bike Road Rally:

This is a simple "treasure hunt" event in which teams of three to four bike riders must follow clues to reach a final destination. By arranging for the teams to go different routes, yet ending up at the same place, they won't be able to follow each other. The first team to finish the course is declared the winner. This should take about an hour.

Bike Tour:

Last on the activity list is a bike ride to a not-too-distant park or beach for a hamburger or hot-dog feed.

BICYCLE RODEO

Here is another collection of bike games which can be included in an all day bicycle outing for your youth group:

1. *Calf-Roping:* Have one kid stand in the center of an open area and each contestant tries to "rope the calf" as he rides by on a bycycle. After a rider successfully "lassos" the person in the middle, he should immediately drop the rope to avoid injury to himself or the "calf." The calf may duck, but he must keep his hands at his side and stay on his feet. Fastest time wins.

2. *Bull Dogging:* This is rough. Have some big guys play the bulls. (Have them use football gear if they have it.) The cowboys and bulls line up about 10 feet apart. When the whistle blows, the bull runs straight out. The cowboy goes after him. Cowboy jumps from bike and tries to bring the bull down. The bull tries to keep going on his feet as long as he can. Use old bikes, as they could possibly be damaged. This game should not be played on pavement or hard ground. Fastest time wins.

3. *The 100-Yard Crawl:* Bikes must travel in a straight line to finish line 100 yards away. The idea is to go as *slow* as possible. If a rider touches a foot or any part of his body to the ground (trying to maintain his balance) or goes off course, he is disqualified. The last person to finish wins.

4. *Bike Cross Country:* This is an obstacle course race that can include anything you want. The rougher the better. From a starting point, bikes compete for time. On the trail have a "long jump" (4 inch log that the bike must jump over). "Tight rope" (a 2 x 6, 12 ft. long about 6 inches off the ground). A "Limbo Branch" (low tree branch or board about 10 inches above the handle bars). "Tire Weave" (8 or 10 old tires set up in a row about 6 ft. apart). The one to complete the course in the fastest time wins. You can make penalties for those who mess up on some of the obstacles.

5. *100 Yard Sprint:* This is a regular 100 yard dash from a stand-still with bikes.

6. *Bike Pack:* See how many can fit on a bike and still go 10 feet.

7. *Bicycle Demolition:* Have all bike riders form a large circle. Need about 100 feet diameter. They may each have all the water balloons they can carry. (Stuffed in shirts, pockets, etc.) When the whistle blows, they all interweave in the circle and let each other have it!

CRAZY CREATIVE SCAVENGER HUNT

Here's a fun variation of the old scavenger hunt. Give each team a list of crazy names (such as the following sample list) and the kids have to go out and collect items that they think *best fits* the names on the list. For example:

1. APBJ
2. Zipper zapping shoestring fuse
3. Idaho
4. Tweed
5. Snail Egg
6. Chicken Lips
7. Will be
8. Pine Needle Bushing Brush
9. Snipe
10. Piano Key Mustache Waxer
11. G-Branded Breast Boxers
12. Yellow Grot Grabber
13. Portable Electric Door Knob Kneeler
14. Thumb Twiddly Dummer
15. Thingamabob
16. An Inflatable Deflater
17. Galvanized Goul Gooser

A panel of judges can determine the winners based on each team's explanation of how their "items" fit the various descriptions on the list.

FOTO-MAP

Here's a great variation of the old "treasure hunt" which is not only different, but lots of fun. It works just like the normal treasure hunt—that is, the players all leave at the same time, and go from clue to clue (location to location) in search of the "treasure." The group that gets to the treasure first wins.

"Foto-map" is played similarly, except that the "clues" are photographs. At the starting place, each group or team receives a photograph. The photo is a picture of the first clue location and the group must identify that location by looking at the picture.

Obviously, you can make these photos either easy to recognize or almost impossible to recognize. Each group should be traveling by car (or bikes, etc.) and they might have to just drive around until they spot something that looks like their picture. When they figure it out, they go to the location pictured and there they are given the next photo. A good game can consist of anywhere from five to ten clue locations, depending on their difficulty. The group that arrives at the final destination first is the winner. You might give each group a sealed envelope revealing the final destination in case they haven't reached it before a specified time. Before that time, each group must turn in that sealed envelope in order to win.

FRISBEE FROLICK

For this special event, all you need is an open field and a few "Frisbees" (available everywhere). Divide the group into teams and play the following Frisbee games:

1. *Distance Frisbee:* Line teams up in columns behind a line and each player gets three throws for distance. After each person throws the Frisbee, a judge marks the spot. The thrower retrieves the Frisbee for the next person in line. Farthest throw and the first team to finish (best combined total) wins.

2. *Accuracy Frisbee:* The teams stay lined up in their columns behind the line and a tire is set upright about 25 feet away from each team. One by one, the team members try to toss the Frisbee through the tire. Again, they retrieve their own Frisbee and return it to the next person in line. The most successful throw wins. Or, each person continues throwing until successful, and the first team to finish wins.

3. *Team Toss Frisbee:* Line up two teams opposite each other about twenty feet apart. The first person on one team throws to the first person on the other team who tosses the Frisbee back to the second person on the first team, who throws it back to the second person on the second team, and so on. (See diagram.) The thrower's team scores a point if the catcher drops the Frisbee and the catcher's team scores a point if the thrower tosses the Frisbee beyond the reach of the catcher who must keep his feet planted. There should be a neutral judge for each game. You can play to a certain score or until everyone has thrown the Frisbee four or five times.

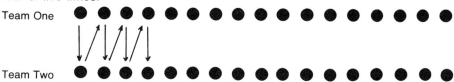

4. *Crazy Legs Frisbee:* The teams line up in columns behind a starting line and there is a finish line 20 feet away. Each team has one Frisbee. The first person places the Frisbee between his knees and runs to the finish line where he tosses the Frisbee back to the next person. If the Frisbee is not caught, the thrower must go back and do the whole routine all over again. First team with all its members across the finish line wins.

5. *Frisbee Water Brigade:* Teams are lined up in columns behind a starting line; each team has a Frisbee (should be the same size for each team), and large pan of water by the starting line, and a wide mouth quart jar about 20 feet away. The object is to get as much water in the jar as quickly as possible by carrying it in the Frisbee. The team that fills the jar the most times in two minutes wins. Obstacles such as chairs to cross, or stairways, etc. add to the fun.

6. *Frisbee Stand-Off:* You need one expendable Frisbee for this one. The object is to get as many people as possible with their feet partially or wholly on the Frisbee or with their weight completely supported by people on the Frisbee. Give them two minutes to practice, and then a one minute period to get the people on. At the end of the time limit, count them. The team with the most on wins.

7. *Freestyle Frisbee:* This is for the "hot dogs." You can have one or two participants from each team demonstrate their best "freestyle" Frisbee throw. This could be around the back, under the leg, over the head, double skip, boomerang, or any other kind of fancy or crazy shot. A panel of distinguished and expert judges determine the winners.

There are also other Frisbee games you can improvise such as "Fris Ball" (Softball played with a Frisbee), or "Frisbee Golf," and all kinds of Frisbee relays.

GUINNESS GAMES

Here's a great idea that can become an annual event for your youth group. Have a day of contests in which kids may try to set a "world's record" a la *The Guinness Book of World Records.* However, kids do not compete against the Guinness book, but against themselves. The first year, "records" are set and the following year kids try to break them, and set new records which last for another year. Here are a few sample contests:

Eating Contests (Amount of food eaten within time limit)

1. Hamburgers
2. Tacos

3. Sloppy Joes
   4. Marshmallows
   5. Lemon Wedges
   6. Onions
   7. Bananas

Endurance Contests (Time)

   1. Standing on your head
   2. Running in place
   3. Talking
   4. Stare down
   5. Pogo Stick jumping
   6. Dribbling a basketball
   7. Keeping eyes open without blinking

Skill Contests

   1. Free throw shooting (percentage of shots)
   2. Frisbee throwing (distance)
   3. Marshmallow throwing (distance)
   4. Burping (number in succession)
   5. Bubble blowing (number in succession)
   6. Various games (highest score)

Other Contests

   1. Volkswagen Stuff (number of kids inside)
   2. Hula Hoop Pack
   3. Marshmallows stuffed in mouth (number)

There should be a separate boys and girls category in the athletic contests. Kids can pay an "entry" fee, and sign up for whichever events they would like to try. "Trophies" can be presented to the new record holders.

HERITAGE DINNER

In order to help kids to get in touch with their own backgrounds and to facilitate communication of this to the other members of the group to get an idea of where each is "coming from," try this variation of the old potluck dinner. Each person is instructed to bring to the event a dish that represents his or her ancestry. Nearly every American has roots in some other nationality, and this could be preceded by a little research into family trees, etc. If a person has many nationalities in his or her background, then one could be chosen. If a person doesn't know of any representative food for his or her ancestry, then more research may be needed.

In addition to the meal, the kids should bring with them a "family treasure" or some relic, photo, or other item of interest that has been passed down through several generations, and be prepared to tell its story. The item need not be valuable except in terms of the story behind it. Another possibility would be to have kids bring baby pictures of themselves that could be posted and have a contest to see who can guess the identity of each picture.

A further extension of this idea would be to have each kid bring or tell about an item that he or she hopes will be passed on to future generations and remembered. You might have each person think of himself as his own grandchild and then talk about "My grandfather. . . ." What kind of a heritage do you hope to leave for your future family? Good discussion and sharing can follow.

LATE GREAT SKATE

Here's one way to put new life into the old roller skating party that used to be so popular. First of all, make arrangements to rent a roller rink for your own private use. Usually you can get one for a flat rate plus skate rentals. Also, make sure you have the freedom to plan your own skating program, rather than being confined to the normal "all skate, couples only, grand march," ad nauseum, kind of thing. You might want to consider an "all night" skate that starts around midnight and goes until dawn. Roller rinks are easier to get at such a ridiculous hour.

The basic idea is to play all sorts of games on skates. Many of the games mentioned in this book can be played on skates, giving them an added dimension of fun. Races, relays, ball games, all can be done on skates. Just be sure that the games are not too rough, to avoid possible injuries.

Some sample roller skating games:

1. *Rag Tag:* Everyone gets a rag that hangs out of his back pocket or hangs out of his pants. On a signal, everyone starts skating in the same direction. The object is to grab someone else's rag without having yours taken by another skater. Once your rag is gone, you are out of the race. Awards are given for most rags grabbed by one person, and for whoever stayed in the longest.

2. *Obstacle Course Relay:* Set up an obstacle course which the skaters must skate through. The first team to have each of its members skate through it (one at a time), is the winner.

3. *Triple Skate:* Have everyone skate around the rink in threes. No passing is allowed. On a signal, the skater in the middle, or on the right or left, moves up to the next threesome. This is good as a mixer.

4. *Scooter Race:* Have one kid down on his haunches who is pushed by another skater. Set a number of laps for the race.

5. *Tumbleweed:* Have all the skaters go down to a squat when the music stops or when the whistle blows. This will tire them quickly.

6. *One-legged Race:* Skaters race, skating with only one skate on. The other foot is used to push.

7. *Run the Gauntlet:* Girls line up in two parallel lines and the boys skate between them with balloons tied to their seats. The girls try to pop the balloons with rolled up newspapers as they skate by. Another way to do this would be to have clothespins (3) fastened to each boy's back, and the girls try to grab the clothespins as the boys skate by. Awards are given to the girl who grabs the most clothespins, and to the boy who lasted the longest.

8. *London Bridge:* Two skaters stand opposite each other, grab hands and form a "bridge" that other skaters can skate under. Each team then lines up and on a signal, begins skating under the bridge. Once under the bridge, each skater circles around and goes through again, as many times as possible before the time limit is up. There should be a counter standing by the bridge, counting the skaters as they

91

pass under the bridge. The team that gets the most skaters under the bridge in the time limit wins.

There are many other possibilities, of course. For breathers, you might want to show some films, serve sandwiches and refreshments, or whatever else you can get away with.

PHONE BOOK BIKE RALLY

For this event, each kid is instructed to bring a phone book and a bike. Kids may also need back-packs or baskets to carry the phone books while riding. A list of locations is passed out to everyone (on separate slips, so that each person will take them in a different order) and each kid must obtain the information asked for. No phone calls are allowed. Each location must be visited. The following list is a sample. You obviously will need to select places in your own city that can be looked up in a phone book. The first person to complete his list within the time limit is the winner. This can also be done in cars.

1. Ed Saldin's Drug Store: *What hours are posted on the front door?*
2. Yo Yo's Cafe: *What number telephone pole is directly behind the building?*
3. Loving Day Care Center: *What kind of animals are on either side of the front door?*
4. San Marco Apartments: *What product is advertised on their sign?*
5. Guthrie Cabinet and Millwork Shop: *How many panes of glass above the sign on the front of the building?*
6. Spratt's Metal Works: *What does the traffic sign directly in front of the building say?*
7. Anderson's Grocery: *What kind of flour is stacked in the front window?*
8. Yakima Ambulance and Towing: *How many trees growing in front of the building?*
9. Hobbit Shoppe Antiques: *Name the farm implement hanging over the front door.*
10. Apple Tree Gift Shop: *The display in the front window features glassware and what?*
11. The Walter J. Farnsworthy home: *What kind of flowers in the front yard?*

5 | Service Projects

BOOK BLAST

Have the youth group write a book. Really tap the creative potential of the group and have the kids write stories, poetry, articles and essays or submit cartoons, drawings, and anything else that can be reproduced. Then have it all edited by a committee, pasted up and printed by the "offset" process. (Photos can be included this way.) A local printer or bindery can bind them into books. Select a catchy title and design a nice cover which can be printed or silk-screened on cover stock. The books can then be advertised and sold in the church and community as a fine fund raising project.

CHRISTMAS LOCK-IN

If you are looking for a significant and meaningful activity for your youth group (ninth grade and above), the Christmas Lock-in is it. The Christmas Lock-in is a 36 hour event that is held one week before Christmas on a Friday and Saturday. Here is the schedule.

Friday:

7:00 P.M. Contemporary Worship Service—run entirely by the kids focusing on the practical meaning of Christmas.

8:00 P.M. Free time for socializing.

9:00 P.M. Doors locked and work begins. Begin by making favors for the nursing home that the kids will be visiting Saturday. Then wrap gifts for poor families and the children at Children's Hospital (or the children's ward of any hospital). After that, pack food baskets for the poor (get the food from a congregational door collection along with funds raised from the youth themselves). The food that is purchased for the food baskets is bought during a midnight shopping spree.

After midnight: The kids sleep in the church.

Saturday:

  8:00 A.M. Breakfast.
  9:00 A.M. Deliver baskets to the poor.
11:30 A.M. Lunch.
  1:00 P.M. Carol singing and favors given out at nursing home.
  3:00 P.M. Carol singing and gifts distributed at Children's Hospital.
  6:00 P.M. Dinner.
  7:00 P.M. Caroling to church members' homes.
  9:00 P.M. Gala Christmas party with lots of singing, fellowship, and close with communion.

DOMINO DROP

By now, we have all seen the incredible domino mazes in which dominoes are placed end to end in a huge design. Then the domino at the beginning of the design is pushed over and one by one the others fall until all the dominoes have fallen. Many of these designs are so intricate that it takes many minutes for all the dominoes to fall.

Have your youth group get people to pledge a certain amount of money per domino. Then have your group design a pattern of dominoes that will include as many dominoes as they can get their hands on. (They, of course, can practice ahead of time to find the best design possible.) When they have finished their final design of dominoes, they push the first one and watch them all fall. All of the fallen dominoes are counted and then multiplied times the pledge for each domino. This can be a great fund raiser and a lot of fun for everyone involved.

FREE CAR WASH

Set up a youth car wash at a local shopping center or filling station as you normally would. However, instead of charging for the wash tickets, *give them away.* Advertise it as a "FREE CAR WASH." Make it clear that there are "no strings attached." Anyone may get his car washed free by the youth of your church simply because it is a gesture of Christian love and friendship.

However, those who care to may make a contribution of any amount they choose. This money can then be used by the youth for a missionary project, a relief agency providing food for famine stricken countries, or other worthy projects.

A sign may be posted at the car wash site similar to this one:

> Your car is being washed by the youth of _____ church for free with no strings attached. It's just one small way for us to demonstrate to you the love of Jesus Christ. Another way we are attempting to share Christ's love is by collecting funds to help purchase food for the hungry. If you would like to help us with this project, your contribution would be greatly appreciated. Thank you and God bless you.

Of course, your version of this sign would depend on what you were raising money for, but it is suggested that you avoid using this to simply increase the coffers of the church building fund or the youth group's social activities fund. You can print this information on the tickets as well, and many people will come prepared to give.

One youth group did this twice and raised a total of $800.00, strictly through contributions received at their free car washes. Pick a good (busy) location, make sure you have plenty of hard-working, friendly kids, and the experience can be very rewarding.

GLEANING PARTY

If your community has public garden plots or is in an area where there are many farms, your group might consider the old custom of gleaning. Going through the fields after the harvest and salvaging that which is ripe and usable. The food which is collected is sorted and then given to an organization which distributes food to the poor.

H.O.P CLUB

H.O.P. stands for "Help Older People," and the H.O.P. Club is a program in which teens and adults work together to assist the elderly with work that they are unable to do for themselves. This should be an on-going ministry as opposed to a one-shot service project type of thing. Skilled adults train the youth to do carpentry, plumbing, wiring, upholstery, or whatever needs to be done, and give direction and supervision while on the job. Younger kids can be involved in such tasks as washing windows and walls, raking leaves, shoveling snow, moving furniture, writing letters, and so on. Many other people who want to be involved, but less directly, can provide financial assistance, etc. The important thing is that it should be well organized, and carried out on a regular basis. Many senior citizens' groups can provide information on where the greatest needs are, and the elderly community can be informed that this service is available at no charge, or at a very low cost, to them.

A program such as this not only provides valuable relief for the elderly who must pay to have this work done, but also gives kids the opportunity to give of themselves in a meaningful way and to build relationships with a segment of society that they often ignore.

PARTY MAKING PARTY

This is a great idea for youth groups that are tired of having parties and tired of helping others. Have your youth group put on a party for those groups you want to help. You could have a Sweethearts' Banquet for an old folks home, or the elderly in your congregation; or an Easter Egg Hunt for an orphanage or special education group; or a Christmas party for underprivileged kids; a Thanksgiving Banquet for underprivileged kids, widows, or college students who are away from home.

PINS FOR MISSIONS

Here's a fund raiser that has been done with great success. Secure the use of a bowling alley and set up a bowling tournament or just an evening of bowling with your young people. The object is to raise money for a worthy cause, which is done by taking pledges from adults and businessmen in the community. Each kid enlists the help of "sponsors" who pledge a certain amount of money (5 cents, 10 cents, 25 cents, or more) for each point scored while bowling. Each kid bowls three games and the total of the points scored in the three games is the number that determines the amount of each sponsor's pledge. In a tournament, the "winners" continue scoring more points, therefore collecting more money for the cause. One group called the event "Pins for Missions" and the money was used for world missions.

POST OFFICE

Here's a seasonal activity for young people to raise money for a Christmas project. Set up a "church post office" to beat inflation and to beat the slow mail service. It can be fancy or just a table. The church members drop their letters to be delivered as they come into the church. They pay either what they would in postage or just give a donation to the "postmaster." The young people sort the mail and give it out to the correct people as they come by to pick up any cards for them. For a good service project, the young people can deliver to the shut-ins and to people that don't come. You might start a "singing telegram" service and have a set fee for it. The money can be used for special Christmas projects or offerings. Once this starts, the church members will be looking for it every Christmas. It seems to promote good will within the church body. More people send cards when they know the money is going toward a good cause.

RAKE AND RUN

Here's a way to involve kids in a ministry to the community which is great if you live in an area where neighborhood trees shed their leaves each fall. Load up all the kids in a bus and "arm" each with a lawn rake. You just go up and down streets and whenever you see a lawn that needs raking, everyone jumps out and rakes all the leaves up. No pay is accepted for any of the work. It is all done in the name of Christ. You might find out the names of shut-ins who cannot rake their own lawns as specific homes to visit. It can be fun and rewarding for the kids. Note: During the Winter, kids can shovel snow in the same way. You can call it "SNOW AND BLOW."

Be sure to join us in our "Rake & Run" Party this Saturday afternoon from 1:00 until 4:00.

Bring a leaf rake. (If you have one.)
Wear old clothes.

We'll ride the bus to various deserving homes and rake their leaves and then run to the next one.

We'll eat too!

Lots of fun while we do something worthwhile for others.

STAY-AT-HOME WORK CAMP

The idea of a work camp is not new, of course, but for many youth groups they simply do not have the resources for the travel and expense required by projects a long way from home. The Stay-At-Home Work Camp combines all the benefits of a work camp without leaving home.

Find a place a few miles out of town where your group can sleep and eat during the whole period of the work camp (4 to 7 days). The work projects themselves are determined by the needs of your own area and can include painting, remodeling, building buildings owned by those on fixed incomes such as elderly, widows, or those without income.

Whatever the project, the youth should raise the money for whatever expenses are involved for materials. You could also have members of the church buy "scholarships" to pay the room and board of each work camper.

To liven up the conference you can plan activities during the evening for the kids themselves like movies, game nights, etc. Also, if you take slides or Super 8 films of the kids working, it makes for quite a program combined with testimonies from the group.

SUMMER CAROLING

One method of bringing joy to people who are sick or shut-in is a summer caroling experience. Youths visit homes to sing songs and perhaps even prepare meals to eat with the residents. This can be incorporated into "slave day" too, and work can be done for the needy. The minister might agree to join with the youth group and administer communion in the homes of people unable to attend church. Cassette tapes and recorders may be taken to bring worship services and messages from friends to those who cannot leave their homes.

WAY OUT WEIGH IN

Divide kids into teams (car loads) and have them draw for street names or areas of town. They then have one hour to try and collect as much canned goods or other non-perishable foods as they can from residents of the area which they drew. The teams report back and weigh-in the food they collected. The team that has the most (by weight) wins a prize of some kind, and all the food is then given to the needy. You may want to restrict this to church members only, rather than soliciting food from strangers, however, if done during the Thanksgiving season, most people are willing to share with others.

6 | Skits

AS THE STOMACH TURNS

Here is an impromptu promotional skit which requires only preparation by the narrator. Select your players and put them in their appropriate places on stage. Instruct the cast to carry out the action suggested by each line of narration read. Read the narration, dramatically and with great pathos. Pause after each line until players have finished the required action.

Players:

Narrator
Lucille Lovelorn (best played by a guy)
Philip Pharpar (holding a picture frame in front of him)
Franklin Pharpar (with ring and phony check)
A door (a person standing using fist as doorknob)
A table (one or two people on their hands and knees)
A telephone (a person sitting on table using arm as receiver)

Props:

A ring
A phony check

The narration:

And now, the _____ present another episode in the continuing life drama, "As the Stomach Turns." Last time, luscious Lucille Lovelorn had spurned Dr. Preakbeak's advances because her precious Philip Pharpar would soon be graduating from

Law School and they would be married.

Today's scene opens with Lucille standing next to the picture of Philip which is hanging on the wall of her apartment.

Lucille is humming a happy tune to herself as she stares wistfully at her beloved Philip.

"Philip, I miss you so much," she says as she caresses his cheek.

"Hurry home to me," she begs.

Then, she kisses his picture passionately.

Suddenly, the telephone rings.

Lucille prances to the table, picks up the receiver and sweetly says, "Hello."

She smiles and says, "Oh, Gladys, it's you."

Then she frowns darkly.

Philip has found someone new. Philip has told Gladys to tell Lucille goodbye forever.

Lucille slams down the receiver angrily and begins to cry. She runs over to the picture of Philip and screams, "You cad." Then she slaps his picture viciously, and begins to cry louder. She takes the picture of Philip and turns it to the wall; and begins to cry louder.

Then she throws herself on the floor and begins to cry louder.

Suddenly, Franklin Pharpar, Philip's younger brother, approaches the door and begins to knock vigorously.

Lucille gets up, straightens her hair and skirt, and jerks open the door.

Franklin enters the room quickly and says, "Lucille, have you been crying?"

"What's it to you, Batface?" pouts Lucille.

Then she slaps him painfully across the face.

Franklin slams the door as viciously as Lucille had slapped him.

"I'm sorry," cries Lucille.

Then she begins to weep upon his shoulder.

"Philip left me," she sobs as she points to the telephone.

"Tommyrot," says Franklin as he steps back quickly.

"He does love you," he says. "He sent me with this for you."

Lucille gives a shriek of joy as she takes the ring from Franklin's hand.

Then she gives Franklin a big hug.

Lucille leaps to Philip's picture and spins it around to face her.

"I love you too, darling," she cooes.

Then she kisses his picture even more passionately than before.

Lucille begins dancing around the room with Franklin.

Suddenly, the telephone rings again.

Lucille hops to the phone and jerks up the receiver.

"Hello, hello, hello," she sings happily.

"Oh, Philip, it's you," she sighs.

But then a frown clouds her face.

He *has* found someone else; they *are* through.

She slams down the receiver and angrily throws the ring to the floor.

Then she whirls and slaps Franklin.

"You are a liar," she screams.

Then she jumps to Philip's picture.

"You are a worthless animal," she shrieks.

Then she slaps his picture mercilessly.

Then she wrenches the picture from the wall, and throws it to the floor.

Franklin drops to one knee and clasps his hands.

"But I love you, my flower," he sings.

"And I have something more valuable than a ring for you, my pet," he says.

Then Franklin pulls a check from his pocket for the amount of _____.

Here is the supreme gift. He wants to pay her way to _____.

Lucille squeals with delight.

"What a lovely thought, darling," she sighs.

They embrace happily.

Then they walk over Philip's picture and out the door to their new life ahead.

THE BIG DATE

Bill and Karen have just met each other after being introduced by common friends. This is the first date for both. They have just arrived at a local restaurant for a meal.

Bill: (*Embarrassed*) Hi, Karen.

Karen:	*(Equally embarrassed)* Hi, Bill.
Bill:	*(Still embarrassed)* Hi, Karen.
Karen:	*(Still embarrassed)* Hi, Bill.
Bill:	Gosh, this is so . . . *(He leaves sentence fioating)*
Karen:	Yes, it is so . . . *(She also leaves the sentence floating)*
Bill:	Karen, eh, have you had many dates before?
Karen:	The only date I've ever had was on August 13th.
Bill:	Oh really, what was that?
Karen:	My birthday. *(Karen then drops her comb on the floor.)*
Bill:	Oh here! I'll get it. *(As he stoops over, he falls down on the floor.)* I guess I fell for that one, but at least I had a nice trip. *(As Bill stands up, he forgets to pick up the comb.)*
Karen:	Oh, Bill, you're so funny! *(suddenly serious)* But would you mind picking up my comb?
Bill:	*(Embarrassed)* Oh yeah, I guess I forgot. *(As Bill squats down, sound effects are heard of his pants ripping. As he reaches behind him to check out what part ripped, he falls backwards from his squatting position over to his back. At that moment a waiter comes to take the order and not seeing Bill, trips over him and falls to the floor.)*
Karen:	Oh my goodness!
Waiter:	*(Regaining composure)* What in the world were you doing on the floor sir? Aren't our seats comfortable enough?
Bill:	Oh no. The seats are just fine. I was just checking to see if the floor was on the level.
Waiter:	*(Unbelievingly)* I don't know about the floor, but are you on the level? *(waiter then notices the rip, and seeing the chance for a pun replies . . .)* By the way sir, something *terrible* has happened to your pants.

Bill:	Yes I know. Isn't that a rip-off? *(Both men stand)*
Waiter:	Well would you like me to do anything?
Bill:	Yea, how about turning your head when I leave?
Waiter:	*(Unbelievingly)* Sure thing . . . Hey, I'll be back in a minute to take your order. *(As waiter leaves, Bill sits back down at the table.)*
Karen:	Bill, I really appreciate your efforts, but my comb is still on the floor.
Bill:	I'm sorry, Karen, but that waiter crushed my ear when he fell on me. What did you say?
Karen:	I said my comb is still on the floor.
Bill:	*(Sheepishly)* Your phone is in the store?
Karen:	No! MY COMB IS ON THE FLOOR!
Bill:	*(Sheepishly)* Oh! I'm sorry. *(Bends down and gets the comb)* Well, we may as well order, there's no use in waiting around.
Karen:	I don't mind waiting. Sometimes I even like to wait around.
Bill:	What?
Karen:	I said, it gives me a lift sometimes to wait.
Bill:	Yea. I like weightlifting too.
Karen:	Oh good-grief. Not to change the subject, but what did you do today?
Bill:	I got things all straightened out.
Karen:	What do you mean?
Bill:	I mean I did my ironing. Aren't you *impressed?*
Karen:	Not a great deal. I did my laundry today.
Bill:	I thought I smelled bleach! But I thought it was just your hair.
Karen:	*(Offended)* Well, I never . . .

Bill:	Well you ought to, I can't stand the color of your hair.
Karen:	BILL! You've hurt my feelings!
Bill:	*(Bashfully)* Oh, I'm sorry. Speaking of laundry, do you know the money changing machines they have in there?
Karen:	Well, not personally, but go ahead.
Bill:	Well I wanted to prove how stupid those machines are, so I put a 5 dollar bill in one and it still gave me change for a dollar. Just to make sure it was no fluke, I put a 10 dollar bill in the next time and it *still* gave me change for a dollar. I bet you never realized how *stupid* those machines are, have you?
Karen:	That doesn't make sense.
Bill:	What do you mean?
Karen:	I mean you lost 13 dollars and you are saying the *machines* are stupid.
Bill:	Well, I only did it for a change.
Karen:	That's what all the money changers are for; a change.
Bill:	That makes sense.
Waiter:	I don't mean to interrupt, but are you ready to order?
Bill:	Huh?
Waiter:	Your order?
Bill:	What?
Waiter:	ORDER, ORDER!
Bill:	What are you, a judge?
Waiter:	I don't know about that, but whenever I go to play tennis I wind up in a court.
Bill:	You ought to get out of that racket.

Waiter:	*(Looks up and states pleadingly.)* Why me? . . . Have you decided what you would like to eat?
Bill:	Yes, I'll take the New York Sirloin steak, baked potato, corn, tossed salad with French dressing and a large Coke. That's all.
Karen:	What about me, Bill?
Bill:	*(Surprised)* Aren't you going to buy your own?
Karen:	Of course not, it's not proper.
Bill:	O.K. O.K. Waiter, she'll have a small Coke.
Waiter:	You're not going too far *overboard* are you?
Bill:	Don't be silly. We're nowhere near water, much less on a ship.
Karen:	You may be right there, but you're *still* all wet. *(Karen then throws her glass of water all over Bill and they exit.)*

KID RINGO

This skit centers around the old west and would be great at a banquet or party where the theme is western. JESSE JONES should be dressed in full cowboy regalia, look mean and wear his guns low. KID RINGO is a *very old* man who is still trying to live by his legend. He should have a big hat, and barely be able to get around.

Narrator:	In the West of the 1880's violent men dictated the only law of the times. Those who carried guns were the powerful—imposing their will upon peaceful men and women. The highest law of the land was written on the barrel of a Colt 44. Often, cruel men preyed upon innocents, taking whatever they wanted. But some-times, men of the gun met each other in battle for prize, posses-sion or reputation. These "Showdowns" were terrible clashes—the poetry of destruction as written by the pen of hate dipped in an inkwell of blood.
Jesse:	*(He stops at stage, takes out his gun, checks it carefully by rotating the cylinder, then holsters it again. He frees his shoul-der and arm muscles by several stretches and shrugs. He then loosens up his hands and cracks his knuckles. Now satisfied that his is ready, he sets himself with a mean look and a slight crouch, hands ready at his guns. He yells.)* Kid! Kid Ringo! I'm callin' you out! *(no answer) (louder)* KID, I know you're in there. It's me, Jesse Jones. You've eluded me long enough. You're goin' to meet me in the street today and the devil in Hades tonight, Kid! *(The door slowly opens and Kid Ringo begins to come out onto the stage. He shuffles slowly up.)*
Kid:	The "devil in hades" huh? You cain't say that in front of all these ladies.
Jesse:	*(Incredulously)* I cain't! Well I just did!!
Kid:	Well, I guess you've got a point there. *(He turns and begins to leave.)*
Jesse:	Where you goin'?
Kid:	Back to watch the girls go by in the hotel lobby.
Jesse:	Why?
Kid:	I don't remember.
Jesse:	Get back here and prepare to throw hot lead. *(He takes a step or two toward Kid and spurs jingle.)*

Kid:	What's that funny noise?
Jesse:	Them's ma spurs. Don't you wear spurs, Kid?
Kid:	Don't wear 'em anymore after the wife died.
Jesse:	Never mind, Ringo, I've killed 37 men and I'm aimin' to make you 38. How many've you killed?
Kid:	Let's see . . . *(Begins to count slowly on hands, then drops down to take off one boot, when he starts taking off second boot, Jesse interrupts.)*
Jesse:	*(Mad)* Nevermind, you old coot, reach for your guns.
Kid:	Wait a minute, I'm not warm yet. *(Kid goes through a warm-up procedure like Jesse, except for the gun. When he tries to crack his knuckles, he is unable to do so for his lack of strength. Finally he puts his hands under his boots and tries to stand up.)*
Jesse:	C'mon Kid, go for your gun.
Kid:	Not so fast. Let's do it the old way. Back to back, we take 5 paces, turn, draw, and fire.
Jesse:	I don't care how I kill you, let's just do it. *(They come together at stage center, turn back to back.)*
Jesse:	Ready? 1, 2, 3, 4, 5! *(He turns and begins to draw . . . but Kid Ringo is still shuffling and beginning to turn around.)* You're not even ready you dumb old coot. Just back away. I'll give you a chance. You can draw first. When I count 3 you go for your gun. OK?
Kid:	OK.
Jesse:	One! Two! Three! *(pause)* Well, go for your gun.
Kid:	I am. *(His hand slowly creeps toward his gun.)*
Jesse:	This is the last chance I'm givin you, Kid. No more stalling, you'd better be ready, cause this time I'm pullin' down on you. Are you loaded?

Kid:	I wish I were.
Jesse:	Naw, I mean the gun, stupid.
Kid:	Wait a minute, I'll see *(He pulls his gun out and twirls the cylinder. The barrel is pointed away toward the front of stage. As he checks the gun, it goes off. One of the spectators on the front row gasps and slides off the chair, clutching his chest.)*
Jesse:	Now you've done it. You've killed an innocent bystander. You're the worst gunfighter I've ever seen. Don't you even know how to use a gun?
Kid:	I didn't mean to do it. . . . I was just checking my gun and it went off. I must have a bad trigger or something. *(He's pointing the gun down and towards Jesse, and it fires. Jesse groans and slumps to the floor toward the Kid so that he's almost at his feet. The Kid is unaware that Jesse has been shot.)* Did it again. I'd better fight you before I shoot all my bullets. *(Turns toward where Jesse stood and squints, trying to see him.)* Where'd he go? Run off like all them others. *(Holsters gun.)* Yup, they all turns to jelly in their boots when they face up to KID RINGO. *(Shuffles offstage.)*